Germany's New Position in Europe

German Historical Perspectives Series
General Editors: Gerhard A. Ritter and Anthony J. Nicholls

Volume I
Population, Labour and Migration in 19th- and 20th-Century Germany
Edited by Klaus J. Bade

Volume II
Wealth and Taxation in Central Europe: The History and Sociology of Public Finance
Edited by Peter-Christian Witt

Volume III
Nation-Building in Central Europe
Edited by Hagen Schulze

Volume IV
Elections, Parties and Political Traditions: Social Foundations of German Parties and Party Systems
Edited by Karl Rohe

Volume V
Economic Crisis and Political Collapse: The Weimar Republic, 1924–1933
Edited by Jürgen Baron von Krudener

Volume VI
Escape into War: The Foreign Policy of Imperial Germany
Edited by Gregor Schöllgen

Volume VII
German Unification: The Unexpected Challenge
Edited by Dieter Grosser

German Historical Perspectives/VIII

Germany's New Position in Europe

Problems and Perspectives

Edited by
ARNULF BARING

BERG

Oxford/Providence, USA

First published in 1994 by
Berg Publishers
Editorial offices:
150 Cowley Road, Oxford, OX4 1JJ, UK
221 Waterman Road, Providence, RI 02906, USA

Library of Congress Cataloging-in-Publication Data

A catalogue record for this book is available from the British Library.

British Library Cataloguing in Publication Data

A catalogue record for this book is available from the British Library.

ISBN 1 85973 091 4 (Cloth)
　　 1 85973 096 5 (Paper)

Printed in the United Kingdom by WBC Bookbinders, Bridgend, Mid-Glamorgan.

Contents

Editorial Preface   vii

Foreword   ix

'Germany, What Now?'
Arnulf Baring   1

Germany's Position in the Centre of Europe: the Significance
of Germany's Position and Misunderstandings about
German Interests
    Günther Gillessen   21

National Interest and International Responsibility: Germany's
Role in World Affairs
    Gregor Schöllgen   35

Europe in a Cul-de-sac
Joachim Fest   51

Germany and Eastern Europe between Past and Future
Jochen Thies   65

German Grand Strategy after the Cold War
Josef Joffe   79

The Power and the Past: Germany's New International Loneliness
Christoph Bertram   91

Germany's National and European Interests
Hans-Peter Schwarz   107

Notes on Contributors   131

Suggestions for Further Reading   133

Editorial Preface

The purpose of this series of books is to present the results of research by German historians and social scientists to readers in English-speaking countries. Each of the volumes has a particular theme which will be handled from different points of view by specialists. The series is not limited to the problems of Germany but will also involve publications dealing with the history of other countries, with the general problems of political, economic, social and intellectual history as well as international relations and studies in comparative history.

We hope the series will help to overcome the language barrier which experience has shown obstructs the rapid appreciation of German research in English-speaking countries.

The publication of the series is closely associated with the German Visiting Fellowship at St Antony's College, Oxford, which has existed since 1965, having been originally funded by the Volkswagen Stiftung, later by the British Leverhulme Foundation, by the Ministry of Education and Science in the Federal Republic of Germany, and, starting in 1990, by the Stifterverband für die Deutsche Wissenschaft with special funding from C. & A. Brenninkmeyer Deutschland. Each volume is based on a series of seminars held in Oxford, which has been conceived and directed by the Visiting Fellow and organised in collaboration with St Antony's College.

The editors wish to thank the Stifterverband für die Deutsche Wissenschaft for meeting the expenses of the original lecture series and for generous assistance with the publication. They hope that this enterprise will help to overcome national introspection and to further international academic discourse and cooperation.

Gerhard A. Ritter   Anthony J. Nicholls

Foreword

This volume consists of lectures given at a seminar which I organised in 1993 and which was held in Hilary Term between January and March 1994 at St Antony's College, Oxford.

I was convinced that Germany's international position had been profoundly transformed after the reunification of the country, and I found the absence of a thorough and consistent national debate in Germany about our future interests and about our country's aims and objectives in foreign policy very surprising, even worrying. Therefore all speakers were asked to elaborate on the question of whether Germany needed a new foreign policy for the coming decades. At the same time I felt that our contemporary problems had to be interpreted in historical perspective.

Anthony Nicholls agreed that these topics were of interest for a British public and, once published, for English-speaking readers.

I am very grateful to St Antony's College for its hospitality, to Anthony Nicholls, Jennifer Law and Anna Lever for all their cooperation and help, and to the *Stifterverband für die Deutsche Wissenschaft* for its financial support which made the lectures and this publication possible.

Arnulf Baring

ARNULF BARING

'Germany, What Now?'

Late last year, I was asked to discuss with a German audience the new international situation as it affected our country. The topic was 'How new is the current German position? (Wie neu ist die deutsche Lage?)' or in other words, to what extent has Germany's international situation changed since 1989/90? The answer is very simple, although the situation is not; the situation is very new and yet very old at the same time.

Germany's situation in Europe is now in many ways completely different from the one which confronted it as the Federal Republic before 1989-90. However, it is not so different from the situation facing Germany between 1871 and 1945. Germany has been united and transported back into the centre of Europe by 'Her Majesty History'[1] as Wladimir Semjonov, for decades a leading specialist on Germany in the Soviet Ministry of Foreign Affairs, remarked to Timothy Garton Ash. Many foreigners thought and still think that this new German position presents enormous opportunities for our country; Fritz Stern has spoken of 'a second chance' for Germany.[2] He pointed out that such a repeat of good fortune was a very rare thing in history, but Germany had achieved it through the unforeseen vagaries of the East European uprisings and revolutions.

However, the Germans themselves are not at all enthusiastic about the new prospects history has opened up for them. They are frightened; they have 'angst', because history has dictated that they are back in precisely that central European position which, to say the least, they did not handle very successfully in the decades between 1871 and the end of the Third Reich in 1945.

'Modern Germany was born encircled',[3] wrote David Calleo a few years ago. In order to understand how this is so, let us remember

1

what the old – indeed very old – German position was and how it changed between 1806, when the Holy Roman Empire of the German Nation was dissolved, and 1871, when the Second Empire was formed, and between 1945, after the destruction of Hitler's Third Reich, and 1990, the year of German reunification.

What is Central Europe today? What was it yesterday, what will it be tomorrow? Charles de Gaulle said that the German problem – and the temporary solutions it finds – is the European problem par excellence,[4] because the German question and its solutions concerns all our neighbours and partners in Europe. For a number of reasons, of which Germany's geographical position in the centre of Europe seems to be the most important, the German question has not found a permanent answer in the last two hundred years.

Germany was, and remains, too weak and at the same time too strong, too weak to shape the continent and too strong to be easily accepted by its neighbours[5] – and Germany has more neighbours than most states in the world. Its location, opportunities and internal and external pressures continuously influence Germany's shape and behaviour. It is a country eternally in transition. But it is also a transit country through which many pass, a country influenced, deeply affected and transformed by all the great movements of religions, cultures and military powers in Europe. Germans have been culturally enriched by this continuous flow of ideas, models and migrant peoples, but they have also been politically and militarily more and more endangered, especially since the development of European nationalist tendencies in the late Middle Ages and the building of national states after the French Revolution.[6]

No German regime of the last two hundred years has lasted long enough to cultivate deep roots in the German mind or to foster lasting traditions; no regime could truly legitimise itself. We are – and perhaps remain for ever – a country of promising beginnings, dramatic changes and abrupt breakdowns. Perhaps we are eternal beginners. Germany is a country with a never-ending series of surprising inceptions and equally surprising finales; it is a deeply disturbed country, unsure of itself. Dolf Sternberger, the famous political scientist from Heidelberg, said in 1949: 'We do not know who we are. This is the German question.'[7] Forty-five years later, after the end of the old Federal Republic, this still seems to be a valid observation.

What are the lessons of the past, what can it teach us about our future chances and risks? As I have already mentioned, there was first of all the old German Empire which lasted until 1806: this was an enormously large country, the biggest territory in Europe except for Russia. Because of its weak internal power structure the Empire was unable to attack, but with important exceptions – it was strong in self-defense:[8] it was in many ways the calm centre of Europe.

After the defeat of Napoleon this old Germany was somehow re-created by the Congress of Vienna in 1815. Can this peace settlement of Vienna tell us something about the future of central Europe in the twenty-first century? Josef Joffe has already raised this question. We have since had two modern European peace orders, that of Paris after 1918 and that of Yalta after the Second World War. The international order created at Yalta collapsed in 1990, and that of St. Germain and Trianon collapsed two years later with the civil war in the former Yugoslavia and the division of Czechoslovakia. Digging further into the past, we discover that the next peace order we find is that which came out of the Congress of Vienna. Perhaps it is a far-fetched idea to go back 180 years; more than half of the European borders have been drawn in the twentieth century. We have a large number, a growing number of new states in east central Europe, and they all – or at least most of them – will also exist in the future. However, where are the alternative orientations, what are the alternative solutions?

One implication of the Vienna model – among many other factors – would be the resurrection of some kind of Austro-Hungarian federation, for which I see some indicators (perhaps only day-dreams) in some of the successor states. After the formation of such a federation, which might include Bohemia, Slovenia, Croatia and Southern Tyrol, another implication would be a possible revival of the old rivalry between Berlin and Vienna. Because of the Prussian-Austrian antagonism which divided Germany against herself before 1806 within the old Empire and within the German Bund after 1815, Germany was unable to exert much influence beyond its borders despite its expansion in size. Because of all its internal divisions it was unable to attack but, as already mentioned, Germany remained strong in defence and was therefore able to neutralise the centre of Europe. In view of the enormous changes in many fields since 1815, a return to the Europe of the Vienna Congress is not very likely to happen, but it is not impossible; what could be the alternatives?

The second German model which comes to mind is the Bismarckian Germany of 1871, a reduced Germany in the same central European position as the former Holy Roman Empire and the Bund, situated between the Poles, the Russians, the Austrians and Hungarians in the East and the French, the British and others in the West. The new Germany created by Bismarck in the course of the 1860s and early 1870s of the last century was much smaller than the old Empire, but was much more united and much more of a force to be reckoned with because she had industrialised herself with enormous speed:[9] within two or three decades Germany transformed herself from a predominantly agricultural country into the position of a leading industrial power in Europe, beginning to compete with the United States. The other European powers accepted the emergence of this new Germany with some reluctance.

In order to stabilise and to calm the fears of neighbouring states, Bismarck proclaimed that Germany was saturated.[10] She desired, he said, no territorial gains and no colonies. Germans living outside the borders of the new Reich of 1871 should give up hope of being reunited one day with their brethren inside Germany. In Bismarck's words Germany had to be the modest, selfless broker of Europe.[11] He felt that Germany should behave in such a way that all her neighbours would regard Germany's existence as being in their own interest. All countries in Europe should come to the conclusion that they needed Germany for their own safety and for the stability of the continent. All countries, and all interests, would be balanced against each other by Germany's helping hand – and of course, only by peaceful means.[12]

At first sight, the Bismarckian programme appears to have been very modest, but in fact it was very ambitious from the beginning. Almost from the beginning, the founder of the Reich faced enormous difficulties in putting this programme into practice.The French were openly opposed because France had lost its position as leading power in Europe, regained, it seemed to the French, under Napoleon III. Even without the annexation of Alsace-Lorraine and the humiliating proclamation of the new Reich at the Royal Palace of Versailles, French resentment would have been strong.[13] It was natural that the French should feel aggrieved at being replaced by the Germans as the leading power in Europe, and in this respect history repeats itself today under very different circumstances: there has been a noticeable re-emergence of French resentment against Germany since 1989, with Paris suspecting that France will lose its dominant position within the European Community to the Germans.

Another problem was Russia. Since the three divisions of Poland, Russia had become a closer and therefore more threatening neighbour of little Prussia, a situation obviously regarded with mixed feelings by the Prussians themselves. However, Russian backing was also a decisive component of Bismarck's success in uniting Germany. In the Russians' mind, therefore, their country was entitled in return to German benevolence and German compensation. Since the eighteenth century, first Prussia and later Germany had been well aware of the growing interest and influence of Russia in the affairs of the continent, especially in the Slavic part of the Balkans.[14] Russian expansionism in the south eastern parts of Europe led to growing friction with Germany, in the beginning not so much because of German economic interests in the Balkans but because of Austrian-Russian antagonism there. Austria *and* Russia both hoped to become heir to the decaying Ottoman Empire. Bismarck was determined to avoid taking sides, but in the end the growing interests of Russia in the Balkans alienated Russia not only from Austria, but also from Germany.

The Congress of Berlin in 1878 has long been regarded by many historians as a triumph of Bismarckian statesmanship.[15] In fact, however, it was the beginning of a deep rift between Germany and Russia which led to the French-Russian rapprochement in the 1880s and to an alliance between these two states in the 1890s. This was the beginning of a very threatening scenario for Germany: it meant the danger of a war on two fronts, in both the east and the west.

Germany could have stabilised the situation in spite of this danger by establishing good relations with Britain, and there were several timid attempts at working towards an understanding between the two countries, if not towards an alliance.[16] From the times of Bismarck to the times of Hitler at least, parts of the German leadership saw the necessity of establishing a better understanding between Germany and Britain. But Britain was not interested in close links with Germany because London was not yet concerned about the dangers of a Franco-Russian alliance against Germany. Britain was the leading world power of the day; there were serious rivalries with both France and Russia, but Britain did not feel seriously threatened by either and London had always been successful in finding temporary solutions each time the conflicts threatened to explode. Certainly a defeat of Germany by a joint assault by France and Russia would have destroyed the European balance of power and one can assume that Britain would have joined forces with Germany at a time of serious crisis in order to stabilise the European situation. But Germany lacked patience to wait for this moment, and in addition alienated the British by building a naval fleet and setting up German colonies in various parts of Africa.

In the early years of his chancellorship Bismarck had seemed quite successful in avoiding the obvious dangers of Germany's central European position. However, in spite of all his experience, intelligence and ability to manoeuvre when the situation required it, the positive results of his strategy were fast diminishing even while he was still in office. After 1890, first Wilhelm II and later, with even more dangerous consequences, Hitler both completely misunderstood the requirements and implications of the Bismarckian creation of the national state. They believed that Germany had no chance of survival unless it remained at all costs an independent great power; they even added that it would have to become a world power in order to secure its existence.

This was a fateful misunderstanding of the requirements of the German location! In my view, Germany could only secure her future at that time by becoming the *junior* partner of Great Britain.[17] Later, after 1949, Germany's role was to become a junior partner of the United States, which had taken over Britain's role in the world during and after the Second World War. The idea of a completely independent Germany, given its geographical situation in Central Europe, was an illusion from the start. It would be an equally unpardonable mistake, a miscalculation of enormous proportions, to attempt such an independent role today or tomorrow. Germany was and is a country with limited resources, limited powers, and many geographical, historical and political weaknesses and shortcomings. We were and remain a second-rate power, a middle-sized country.

A third German model came about as a result of Hitler's defeat: this was Adenauer's Rhenish republic.[18] The Federal Republic was a complete break with the foreign policy traditions of the former Reich. However, this reorientation was due much more to the forceful – and in each case very different – influences of the four-power occupation of Germany than to any intellectual re-examination of our past and the disaster it had left behind. There was no national debate, no new 'grand design'. Perhaps debate or design were not necessary: the results of the dictatorship and its war spoke for themselves.

It was Adenauer who drew the appropriate conclusion on his own initiative. He had always shown his preference for a Germany with a strong pro-Western orientation.[19] Now he had his chance to put into practice what he had envisaged and hoped for as early as the 1920s.

However, his Germany was only the Western half of the greater Germany; the other half had been lost to Poland and to the Soviet orbit. By force of events, what remained free of Soviet domination in Germany was pushed westwards in 1945. It was the genius of Adenauer that as early as the autumn of 1945, earlier than all his fellow politicians, he realised that while in some ways the division of Germany represented an enormous loss, namely the loss of national unity and the enslavement of Germans under the yoke of the Red Army, at the same time it also presented a great opportunity, at least for the West Germans.

Adenauer had always been critical of Bismarck. He admired Bismarck's skilful art of enacting Germany's ambivalent role. But already as a young man he felt that Bismarck's techniques were too complicated and too risky for his successors. Henry Kissinger wrote after Genscher's resignation from the Foreign Ministry in Bonn in 1992 that only two German statesmen of the last one hundred and twenty years had a coherent vision of Germany's role:[20] Bismarck and Adenauer. Bismarck, Kissinger said, relied on his extraordinary aptitude and his skill (*Geschicklichkeit*), while Adenauer attached most importance to reliability (*Verläßlichkeit*). In the same breath Kissinger went on to praise Genscher's skilfulness, a rather questionable compliment in this connection.

Old Germany's inevitable ambivalence, often regarded by others as unreliability, isolated itself from East and West as, for instance, the Rapallo complex has shown. It seems today that Adenauer's integration of the Federal Republic into the West and the decision to transform Germany forever into a purely Western European country was a very wise choice; indeed, the only possible and reasonable choice at the time of the Cold War when the eastern part of the country and the whole of Eastern Europe was shut off by the Iron Curtain.

However, the same choice was less well suited to the era of détente and even less to the era of German and European unification. The slow return of West Germany to the old central European position started with détente. At the same time, all of Germany's historic difficulties of orientation began to reappear. While in the 1950s and 1960s the Federal Republic had had only two major centres of international orientation – Washington and Paris – with the beginning of the *Neue Ostpolitik* after 1969, Eastern European capitals – Moscow in the first place, but also Warsaw and of course East Berlin – also became important points of orientation. David Calleo wrote

in the 1980s that while Bonn always told the French that they were
Germany's most important partners in Europe, because of the
situation of West Berlin and the Soviet military threat, Bonn's
cooperation with Paris could not progress so far as to endanger the
close relationship with the United States.[21]

Even in times of extreme tension between the United States and
the Soviet Union this little Central European détente had to be
preserved at any price. On the other hand, the United States was
told that the vitally important process of Western European
integration would prevent Germany from establishing an exclusive
relationship with America. As soon as Germany had entered the
phase of détente both Paris and Washington were informed that she
could not join forces with the Western partners beyond a certain
point because of the 16 million Germans under Soviet rule. And of
course the Germans told the Soviet Union and her allies that because
of their Western ties, close cooperation was only possible on a limited
basis.

Already in the 1980s, Calleo maintained that the Germans would
not be able to maintain this position of limited partnership and
limited reliability. In the long run, he wrote, they would have to make
a choice. To put it differently, some time before 1989 the Germans
had already moved backward into the old Central European position,
inevitably balancing one important relationship against the others
on a continuous basis. Reunification has increased the chances of
manoeuvering more freely but also, mutatis mutandis, has increased
potential dangers Europeans remember well from the time of
Bismarck, Wilhelm II and Stresemann. Of course, Western
integration will also remain Germany's basic orientation in the
future, but the country has returned to the centre of the continent.

Germany today is different from the old Federal Republic and even
more different from Bismarck's Reich. However, a continuity
between Bismarck and Kohl has been re-created and re-discovered
since 1990. Germany today has above all been remodelled by
Adenauer and his contemporaries, and has been reshaped into a
liberal, open-minded, Western-orientated, free market society. This
transformation was made possible, or at least facilitated by the
events of 1945, 1947 and 1949.

Between 1945 and 1990 most Germans were convinced that all the
dominant features of earlier German history had ended. Something
completely new had started. Both German states had made a
complete break with the past. The idea of a 'zero hour'[22] was

generally accepted. The only difference was that older generations thought of 1945 as the year of rebirth while some of the younger generation felt that this completely new beginning came in 1968 and thereafter.[23]

These zero hour assumptions were revealed as illusions in 1990. In a totally unexpected manner, Germany got back its historical continuity. We are back in the Germany Bismarck created in 1871, although it is no longer the imperial monarchy of one hundred and twenty years ago but a westernised democratic and liberal republic, the new modernised form of Germany created by Adenauer together with his partners and opponents in the decades after 1949. After 1945 Germany no longer existed as a unified nation state, and many were relieved at this. But in 1990 the nation state came back. The new situation facing the country – and the continent – after 1990 resembles much more the constellations of the late nineteenth and earlier twentieth century than the European structure of the last four decades.

Objections could be raised to much of the above. Can one really speak today of a return of the past, especially of such a distant past? The decades after the Second World War have witnessed fundamental changes in the western world. NATO and the European Community (or European Union as it is called today) have developed a degree of integrated cooperation which was unknown in former times. And both institutions, NATO and the EU, still function with most of their acquired efficiency. NATO is still the only effective military alliance the world has seen in a long time. The United States still maintains its commitments and its leadership role within this alliance. And on the European side there is the EU, which in some people's eyes marks the beginning of the end of nation states and perhaps the foundation of a unified European federal state.

However, it seems obvious that both alliances and constructions have suffered a reduction in importance, a loss of strength and a loss of direction and determination since the fall of the Iron Curtain and the (perhaps only temporary) end of East-West confrontation. The United States, heir to the British position of world power, seems increasingly reluctant to engage itself actively in European affairs. Washington seems to refuse more and more the leading role in Europe. But without American leadership there will be no united Europe and no opportunity for joint European actions, because Britain, France and Germany are too divided amongst themselves.

We are growing to realise that more and more of the many Western achievements and institutions of the last decades were the result of the Cold War rather than a growing similarity and cohesion between Western countries. With the disappearance of the immediate Russian danger, tensions within the West will build up again. 'Does *the* West still exist?' Owen Harries asked recently,[24] coming to the conclusion that a unified West had only existed as long as the Soviet Union threatened all Western nations equally and collectively.

If it is true that NATO is weakened because of the new international situation in the early 1990s, it is even more true of the European Community (or European Union). Both organisations have created defense communities in times of crisis as in the past when there was a danger of one state dominating the others inside or outside Europe: recent examples include Stalin and his successors, and before them there were Napoleon and Hitler. The European Community was always merely a defence community of the well-to-do, a community for joint economic development; until this day it has remained a community of predominantly economic interests.

The European Community was able to concentrate on economic interests because it was always protected militarily by the United States and, strangely enough, by the Soviet Union, which by means of the Iron Curtain, kept the poor Eastern Europeans apart from their richer western brothers. Within this temporary and artificially created Western European zone of economic cooperation, (the western part of Yalta Europe), France has been the political centre from the very beginning in 1950, and the Brussels bureaucracy has been predominantly an agency of French influence. In view of the situation in 1945 and the following years, with a divided Germany wrestling with the burdens of Hitler's failures and crimes, Bonn was not in a position to become a leading power in Europe. Therefore the West German government accepted the French leadership role and revived memories of Charlemagne's empire.

A Germany completely and exclusively integrated into the West was inevitably the new form of existence. The recent past of Germany, including all the centuries between the ninth and the twentieth century up to 1945, now became irrelevant. The West Germans decided to create a new society, a new nation in its early stages. Even today, for many Germans the notion of the zero hour totally separates contemporary Germany from its history before 1945. As mentioned earlier, the West Germans of today are very nervous about recent developments inside and around the country because they fear Germany will be pushed back into the continuity of German history from which the Western half happily escaped after 1945.[25]

The one-sidedness of the European Community, and its exclusively economic orientation, appears today to be an enormous weakness. The EC (or EU) has never tried to advance ideas, never really promoted a community of values, and never tried to win emotional support in Europe which transcends the purely economic interests of the community. The notion of Europe has always remained very abstract and was never discussed. There has never been a widespread and serious debate in Western Europe on shared values, on a common culture, or on the determining spiritual and cultural factors in a united Europe. From its inception until the present day there have been no European parties or collective European public opinion, only national parties, national public opinion, national newspapers, and, by and large, only national electronic media.

It is possible that the Catholic legacy of France, Italy and Spain still provides a solid base and motivating force which aids the European integration process in these countries, while Protestant countries like Britain or Denmark, not to mention Norway, are less inclined to merge into any supra-national unit, being used to independent national churches. The old Federal Republic, on the other hand, being half Catholic and half Protestant, was somewhere in between these two camps. Because of strong Catholic influence in the Bonn leadership after 1949 Germany leaned – and leans still – towards the Catholic position. But this position will change; united Germany is certainly no longer a society with a solid Catholic background and basis.

Since there was never a discussion within the community about the 'natural' borders of Europe or the unifying factors inside Europe one was never able to reason why Turkey should become a member of the community but not Israel, which is the cradle of European civilisation. Nobody argues whether and why Russia or the Balkan states should become members of the community at some distant future date. It is more obvious today than it was before 1990 that Europe consists of many different nations inside and outside the EU and of many peoples all with their own special traditions and memories. Nation-states are the basis of all European cooperation. Under favourable circumstances they will perhaps one day become members of a European confederation. A greater unity than the cooperation which would result from a confederation would be neither possible nor desirable.

The most important challenge for Germany created by the new situation after 1990 concerns Eastern Europe and the Soviet Union. All Europeans, but Germans in particular, have had to rediscover the East: Eastern Germany, Eastern Europe and all the territories which stretch from the Bug river to the Bering Sea. Germany is the only Western country that borders the former Soviet Block. Russia is no longer a possible conservative ally as she was in the nineteenth century – indeed, only very few in Germany think of Russia as an ally – but neither is Russia, for the time being, the enormous military threat it was as the Soviet Union. However, Russia is threatening Germany in a new way. Should chaos develop there, Russia might be confronted with millions of refugees. If on the other hand some kind of restoration of the old regime was to take place in Moscow, or even if some kind of military threat was to reappear and if a new imperialism and expansionism was to gain a foothold, this would endanger Germany first of all among the Western powers.

François Furet called the Germans and the Russians the two European peoples who squandered their opportunities in the twentieth century.[26] But their fate is even more closely connected; the Soviet Union profited more than any of the other victors from the German downfall of 1945. Now in return, Germany has the best opportunity of becoming the heir to Soviet influence in Eastern Europe – at least, that is what many people in the Eastern part of Europe expect. But it has to be remembered that Germany also runs the greatest risks. To support an effective reconstruction of the territories of Eastern Europe west of the former Soviet Union would far exceed German capacities. Western research institutes have come to the conclusion that 420 billion dollars per year are needed for the reconstruction of Eastern Europe, not including the former Soviet Union. In comparison, the Marshall Plan amounted to the sum of 3.1 billion dollars per year (equivalent to 16.4 billion in today's terms) for the whole of Western Europe. And Eastern Europe is in much better shape than the CIS states. Indeed as Jochen Thies wrote recently, 'A large zone of (possible) turmoil stretches from Germany's Eastern border right up to Vladivostock.'[27] In short we are back in the old dilemmas, which appear today in new forms; it is not the strength, but the weakness of the former Soviet bloc which is threatening today. Or, as has recently been remarked: 'Yesterday they tried to force us by means of their Kalashnikovs, today they use the beggar's hat!'

Since means are limited, especially in this time of deep recession, the Germans have had to concentrate on their immediate neighbours, Poland and the former Czechoslovakia. The stabilisation of the former Soviet Union is completely beyond Germany's abilities, even if it were to join forces with its Western partners. Even a cooperation between France, Britain and Germany would have limited means, but will Britain and France join forces with Germany in attempting what is possible in Eastern Europe? Up to this point, it seems doubtful. German activities in Eastern Europe are regarded by its Western European neighbours with some suspicion. France and Britain have rediscovered old feelings of rivalry against Germany which were more or less forgotten during the Cold War. The French especially are convinced that Germany will gain more from the new situation in Europe than France. In Paris it is suspected that Germany is pursuing a long-term and far-sighted strategy which has more to do with the *Drang nach Osten* than with the desire to deepen ties with the West. In the long run this suspicion could well be justified, wrote Daniel Vernet recently, if France decides to leave the Germans alone to deal with all the problems of post-communism in Eastern Europe.[28] Vernet argued that both governments, the French and the German, appear equally unable to develop concepts for the 1990s which deal with the most urgent problems in the whole of Europe.

Vernet believes that the Germans are still puzzled by the new situation in Europe and are at a loss as to how to grasp their future opportunities and duties. But the French know better. Peter Schmidt recently explained convincingly the thinking behind their calculations.[29] French foreign policy apparently follows guidelines which adapt the still dominant Gaullist tradition to the new situation which has emerged in Europe, in order to secure a leading role for France at a time when Germany's power is seemingly growing and the French are feeling increasingly pushed into the Western corner of the continent. The first principle is, according to Schmidt, a tireless effort to reduce American influence in Europe. France would like to prohibit bilateral relations between individual Western European countries (like Britain and Germany) and the United States because they weaken the overall power position of Paris in the European hierarchy. The second principle is the determination to slow down the process of enlargement of the European Union as long as possible.

Two factors influence this calculation. One is the growing inner weakness of the EU and the increasing difficulty of reaching decisions in view of the growing number of member states. Already before 1989 the Western European Community had lost in cohesion and power. The original six members of the community were all similar in their political and social fabric. They were more cohesive than the new community of twelve which emerged in the 1970s and 1980s. And the process of weakening the EU by enlargement will continue; the diversity of interests, of stages of development, and of perspectives, will increase. Regionalisation of the EU will inevitably take place. Western Europe, Southern Europe, Northern Europe, Eastern Europe, Central Europe have very different geographical locations, face different problems and live under different economic and social conditions. Inevitably a community of twenty-four or thirty member states will be a much less coherent group than the community which exists now, not to mention the original community.

The second factor explaining the reluctance of the French to enlarge the community in the near future is their apprehension that it will see German influence grow in Europe. France assumes that new Eastern European community members would seek close cooperation with Germany and would therefore contribute to an increase of German power within the European Union. The determination to limit Germany's influence was a strong motive behind the French strategy which led to the Maastricht treaty. Schmidt also describes a third aspect of French policies; the French are trying to construct the European Union in a contradictory manner in that they wish to use the potential of their European partners for their own benefit while maintaining French national identity and French freedom of action as far as possible. France wants to preserve her own specific resources – for example the Force de Frappe or the permanent seat in the Security Council – longer than any other European country, while those other countries then have to give up their resources as early as possible – for example the Germans would give up the Deutschmark and the independent Bundesbank. This strategy again was very successful during the process which led to the Maastricht Treaty. Accordingly, a number of observers have come to the conclusion that France had strengthened her position, despite the potentially adverse developments after 1990 which one might have assumed would have weakened the French international position.

What are the consequences and the practical conclusions of what has been outlined? The present German Chancellor, who has often

called himself Adenauer's grandson, sticks to one position he believes
was the essence of Adenauer's foreign policy: France first. In his
opinion France is by far the most important partner of Germany.
Therefore Chancellor Kohl has been willing more than once to agree
to French proposals which went against German interests, especially
in the case of the monetary union, the most important German
sacrifice in the Maastricht Treaty. But besides the great economic
risks involved in the merger of currencies, Kohl has also missed the
psychological aspect of the issue. The Deutschmark is not only a
currency, it is a symbol of German self-confidence. Germans – unlike
the British or the French – are short of national symbols.

Thus, as a result of Kohl's and Mitterand's misconceptions, the
Maastricht Treaty was not a new beginning for the whole of Europe
but the final stage of the past phase of European cooperation. The
process of integration is stagnating, for a number of reasons. In the
end the enlarged European Union will remain what it is now, a
common market useful for all Europeans. In my view, the United
States is much more important for Germany than is France. I feel
that the future belongs to a close cooperation of Washington,
London, and Bonn/Berlin, not only for security reasons, which
remain important in view of recent developments in Russia, but also
to give essential backing to German initiatives in Eastern Europe.

Germany's image in Eastern Europe, which saw enormous
atrocities half a century ago, has shifted in recent years from a
nightmare to a model. But we could easily be shifted back to the
nightmare because of many feelings of ambivalence towards
Germany. Support for Germany by the United States and Britain in
Eastern Europe would be an enormous help and guarantee of success
for all partners involved in this area. We need a joint effort, for
political, psychological, economic and historical reasons. But the
United States is also very important for the domestic stability of the
Germans. The United States is much more powerful than Germany;
it is not afraid of Germany and it never feels threatened by Germany.
Germans, with all their feelings of insecurity and recent failures,
need a partner who is more powerful than themselves. Germany has
learnt from the conflicts which led to two World Wars where both
times its only partners were weaker than herself; the temporary
alliance with Japan was a misunderstanding and a miscalculation on
both sides. The single most important lesson of our history is that
Germany needs a partner who is stronger than Germany in order to
overcome the deep feeling of insecurity which lead in reaction to

German outbursts of aggression. American encouragement, support and control would mean a more balanced image both at home and abroad for the Germans and a more balanced role, especially in Eastern Europe.

In a recent book[30] written by a number of young German political scientists and journalists, many of them born in the 1950s and 1960s, the editors wrote in their introduction: 'In view of the new international situation and the need for German re-orientation, the first important question Germans have to answer is the question of Germany's position in relation to the West.' This seems very surprising and puzzling. First of all, Germany is part of the West, and this is the most important positive outcome of all the decades which have passed since 1945. Secondly, during these decades the Germans always felt that it was Bonn's most important task to keep the alliance together, to minimise the differences of opinion between Paris, Washington and London and to increase all opportunities of compromise between these four countries. Germans were always willing to sacrifice time, energy and money for this purpose since they were the youngest member in the club. We should continue along these lines because the unity of the West remains an important goal in times of turmoil.

Now, it is not so much the West we have to think about as the East. The former GDR, Poland and the Czech Republic, all of Eastern Europe, the former Soviet Union: all these territories and countries will deeply influence Germany. What is the situation in each of these different countries? In what direction will these countries develop? How can we support reasonable changes for the better, and how can we prepare ourselves for the worst? These are the most important new questions which we have to consider carefully, and to answer in a responsible manner. German solutions to these most important new challenges will, as a second step, then lead to German efforts and German initiatives to win the support of our Western allies for joint activities in Eastern Europe. It is in Germany's interest to bring Westernised countries, new liberal democracies and market economies like Poland and the Czech Republic into NATO and the European Union, as soon as possible and not several decades from now, because that would be too late, with perhaps catastrophic consequences.

The new shape of European politics should consist of a more modest, less ambitious European Union, a continuation of NATO which means a strong US-British-German alliance: and an increased

German international responsibility. This last requirement will take
time to materialise. The transformation of Germany will require the
patience and encouragement of her three most important Western
partners.

Notes

1. Wladimir Semjonov in Timothy Garton Ash, *Im Namen Europas.
   Deutschland und der geteilte Kontinent*, München/Wien, 1993, p. 531.
2. Fritz Stern in Udo Wengst (ed.), *Historiker betrachten Deutschland. Beiträge
   zum Vereinigungsprozeß und zur Hauptstadtdiskussion* (February 1990–June
   1991), Bonn/Berlin, 1992, p. 139. According to Timothy Garton Ash the
   notion of the 'second chance' was first mentioned at Chequers where
   Margaret Thatcher convened a number of experts on Germany, among
   them Timothy Garton Ash and Fritz Stern; see Garton Ash, p. 793.
3. David Calleo, *The German Problem Reconsidered: Germany and the World Order
   1870 to the Present*, London, 1978, p. 206.
4. See The Press Conference of the French President Charles de Gaulle,
   on 4 February 1965, in: *Europa-Archiv* 20, 1965, p. 94.
5. Germany's precarious situation as a 'demi-hegemon' in Europe was first
   described by Ludwig Dehio, 'Deutschland in der Epoche der
   Weltkriege', in Dehio, *Deutschland und de Weltpolitik im 20. Jahrhundert*,
   Frankfurt a.M., 1961, p. 13. Jochen Thies and Hans-Peter Schwarz have
   recently followed up on Dehio's comments and applied them to the
   external situation of the reunited Germany; see Jochen Thies,
   'Perspektiven, deutscher Außenpolitik', in Rainer Zitelmann, Karlheinz
   Weißmann and Michael Großheim (eds), *Westbindung. Chancen und
   Risiken für Deutschland*, Berlin, 1933, p. 524, and Hans-Peter Schwarz,
   'Deutsche Außenpolitik nach der Vereinigung', in P. Haungs, K.M. Graß
   and H.-J. Veen (eds), *Civitas*, Paderborn, 1992, pp. 483–506.
6. Germany's awareness of this threat is well treated in Gregor Schöllgen,
   *Die Macht in der Mitte Europas. Stationen deutscher Außenpolitik von Friedrich
   dem Großen bis zur Gegenwart*, München, 1992, pp. 11–31.
7. The complete passage reads: 'Wir wissen nicht wer wir sind. Das ist
   die deutsche Frage. Es gibt nahezu nichts, kein Ziel, keine Form des
   gemeinsamen Lebens, die hier mit ganzem Herzen ergriffen und
   ausgebildet werden könnte. Auf jeder möglichen Gestalt deutschen
   Daseins liegt ein Schatten.' Dolf Sternberger, 'Die deutsche Frage', in
   Herman Glaser (ed.), *Bundesrepublikanisches Lesebuch*, München/Wien,
   1978, p. 275.
8. See also Michael Stürmer, *Die Grenzen der Macht. Begegnung der Deutschen
   mit der Geschichte*, Berlin, 1992, p. 22.
9. See Wolfgang Zorn, 'Industrialisierung und soziale Mobilität in

Deutschland 1861–1914', in *Deutschland und Rußland im Zeitalter des Kapitalismus 1861–1914*, Wiesbaden, 1977, pp. 123–135; Zorn, 'Die wirtschaftliche Integration Kleindeutschlands in den 1860'er Jahren und die Reichsgründungszeit 1850–1870', in *HZ* 197, 1963, pp. 314–132; F.W. Henning, *Die Industrialisierung in Deutschland 1800–1914*, Paderborn, 1979; G. Hohorst, *Wirtschaftswachstum und Bevölkerungsentwicklung in Preußen 1816 bis 1914*, New York, 1977.

10. Bismarck used this famous phrase in 1871 immediately after the conclusion of the Treaty of Frankfurt; see Lothar Gall, *Bismarck. Der weiße Revolutionär*, Frankfurt a.M., 1980, p. 503.

11. Bismarck's address in the Reichstag, 19 February 1878, in Horst Kohl (ed.), *Die politischen Reden des Fürsten Bismarck 1847–1897. Historisch-kritische Gesamtausgabe* (14 vols.), vol. 7, p. 92.

12. See Bismarck's 'Kissinger Diktat', June 1877, in Johannes Lepsius et al (eds), *Die große Politik der europäischen Kabinette von 1871–1914. Sammlung der diplomatischen Akten des Auswärtigen Amtes*, vol. 2, Berlin, 1922–1927, pp. 153–154. It was Bismarck's strategy to avoid a central European war at any cost by diverting tensions from the centre to the periphery. However, there he was prepared to accept aggressive or even bellicose policies as inevitable. See Andreas Hillgruber, 'Kontinuität und Diskonintuität in der Deutschen Außenpolitik von Bismarck bis Hitler' *Großmachtpolitik und Militarismus im 20. Jahrhundert*, Düsseldorf, 1974, p. 18.

13. See Andreas Hillgruber, *Bismarcks Außenpolitik*, Freiburg i. Br., 1981, and Eberhard Kolb, *Der Weg aus dem Krieg. Bismarcks Politik im Krieg und die Friedensanbahnung 1870/71*, München, 1990. For a different interpretation see Wolfgang J. Mommsen, *Großmachstellung und Weltpolitik*, Frankfurt a. M., 1993, p. 14.

14. Any kind of Russian intervention in central Europe was viewed extremely suspiciously in Germany ever since Russian troops had operated in Pommerania in 1711. Then they had been called in by the Prussian king and other German princes to counter Swedish expansion. Later, the feeling of suspicion was further aggravated by Russia's role in the Seven Years War and during the Napoleonic wars. For this see Hans-Peter Schwarz, 'Europas Aufgabe -Neuordnung nach dem Ende der Sowjetunion', in *Forum für Deutschland: Eine neue Weltordnung* (10–12 March 1993 in Berlin), 1993, p. 92. The entire German revolution of 1848 was somewhat overcast by the permanent fear of a Russian intervention. Compare with Thomas Nipperdey, *Deutsche Geschichte 1800–1866. Bürgerwelt und starker Staat*, München, 1993, p. 623.

15. Imanuel Geiss, 'Der Berliner Kongreß – Eine historische Retrospektive', in R. Melville and H.-J. Schröder (eds), *Der Berliner Kongreß von 1878. Die Politik der Großmächte und die Probleme der*

Modernisierung in Südosteuropa in der zweiten Hälfte des 19. Jahrhunderts, Wiesbaden, 1982, pp. 31–49; Geiss, Berliner Kongreß. 13. Juni bis 13. Juli 1878, in Karl O. Freiherr von Aretin (ed.), *Bismarcks Außenpolitik und der Berliner Kongreß*, Wiesbaden, 1978, pp. 69–105; Theodor Schieder, 'Europäisches Staatensystem und Gleichgewicht nach der Reichsgründung', in Aretin, *Bismarcks Außenpolitik*, pp. 17–40.

16. See Friedrich Meinecke, *Geschichte des deutsch-englischen Bündnisproblems 1890–1901*, Berlin, 1927, and P.M. Kennedy, 'German world policy and the alliance negotiations with England 1897–1900', in *Journal of Modern History* 45, 1973, pp. 605–625.

17. See for instance H.W. Koch, 'The Anglo–German alliance negotiations: missed opportunity or myth?', in *History*, vol. 54, 1969, pp. 378–392. Andreas Hillgruber considers the feasibility of a German junior-partnership. He concludes that this was incompatible with the national self-image of Welhelmine Germany for it would have meant a retreat to the second rank of powers; see Andreas Hillgruber, *Deutschlands Rolle in dr Vorgeschichte der beiden Weltkriege*, Göttingen, 1986, pp. 21–22.

18. See Hans-Peter Schwarz, *Vom Reich zur Bundesrepublik. Deutschland im Widerstreit der Außenpolitischen Konzeptionen in den Jahren der Besatzungsherrschaft 1945 bis 1949*, Neuwied, 1980, pp. 423–479; Schwarz, 'Das außenpolitische Konzept Konrad Adenauers', in Rudolf Morsey and Konrad Repgen (eds), *Adenauer-Studien* I, Mainz, 1971, pp. 71–108; Neuwied, *Adenauer. Der Aufstieg: 1876–1952*, Stuttgart, 1986, pp. 617–956; Neuwied, *Adenauer. Der Staatsmann: 1952–1967*, Stuttgart, 1991; Arnulf Baring, *Außenpolitik in Adenauers Kanzlerdemokratie. Bonns Beitrag zur Europäischen Verteidigungsgemeinschaft*, München/Wien, 1969.

19. See for instance Karl Dietrich Erdmann, *Adenauer in der Rheinlandpolitik nach dem Ersten Weltkrieg*, Stuttgart, 1966; Henning Köhler, *Adenauer und die rheinische Republik. Der erste Anlauf 1918–1924*, Opladen, 1986.

20. Henry A., Kissinger, 'Germany's Master Builder', in *Newsweek*, May 25, 1992, p. 15.

21. David Calleo, 'Amerika wird nicht immer der Beschützer sein. Deutsche Vergangenheit und europäische Zukunft', in *Frankfurter Allgemeine Zeitung*, 8 September 1987, p. 8.

22. See Sebastian Haffner, 'Der Erfolg des Grundgesetzes', in Haffner, *Im Schatten der Geschichte*, Stuttgart, 1985, pp. 192; Jürgen Kocka, '1945. Neubeginn oder Restauration', in Carola Stern and Heinrich-August Winkler (eds), *Wendepunkte deutscher Geschichte 1848–1945*, Frankfurt a.M., 1979, pp. 141–168; see also Anselm Doering-Manteuffel, 'Deutsche Zeitgeschichte nach 1945', in *VfZ* 41, 1993, pp. 24–29, who also provides an excellent summary of recent research.

23. See Gerd Langguth, *Die Protestbewegung in der Bundesrepublik Deutschland 1968–1978*, Köln, 1978, pp. 277–286. A critical view of the notion of a

new 'zero hour' can be found in Hermann Rudolph, Mehr als Stagnation und Revolte. Zur politischen Kultur der sechziger Jahre, in Martin Broszat (ed.), *Zäsuren nach 1945. Essays zur Periodisierung der deutschen Nachkriegsgeschichte*, München, 1990, pp. 141–151.

24. Owen Harries, 'Der Zusammenbruch des Westens', in *Europäische Rundschau* 21, 1993 (4), p. 31; see also *Does 'the West' Still Exist? – A Conference of the Committee for the Free World*, New York, 1990.

25. See also Gregor Schöllgen, *Angst vor der Macht. Die Deutschen und ihre Außenpolitik*, Frankfurt a.m., 1993, p. 9.

26. François Furet, 'Das Rätsel eines Zerfalls', in *Schweizer Monatshefte* 71, 1991 (2), p. 117.

27. Jochen Thies, 'Perspektiven deutscher Außenpolitik', in Rainer Zitelmann, Karlheinz Weißmann and Michael Großheim (eds), *Westbindung. Chancen und Risiken für Deutschland*, Berlin, 1993, p. 528.

28. Daniel Vernet, 'Ohne Fantasie', in *LIVING* 6, 1993 (4), p. 28; Vernet, *Was wird aus Deutschland?*, Bergisch Gladbach, 1993, p. 189.

29. Peter Schmidt, 'Frankreichs Ambitionen in der Sicherheitspolitik', in *Außenpolitik* 44, 1993 (4), pp. 335–343.

30. Rainer Zitelmann, Karlheinz Weißmann and Michael Großheim (eds), *Westbindung. Chancen und Risiken für Deutschland*, Berlin, 1993.

GÜNTHER GILLESSEN

Germany's Position in the Centre of Europe: the Significance of Germany's Position and Misunderstandings about German Interests

In 1822, at the Congress of Verona, the system of Conference diplomacy created by Metternich and Castlereagh came to an end. It is claimed that the British Foreign Secretary, George Canning, rejoicingly remarked: 'Thank heavens we're back to the old system: every nation for itself and God for all of us.' What Canning disliked was not so much the result of conference diplomacy but the method of multilateral negotiation and decision-taking. Neither Canning nor British public opinion thought Britain should be bound by resolutions of European congresses beyond Waterloo and the Vienna Final Act.

Europe gradually returned to the old system of case-by-case alliances. But the notion of Europe being a 'concert' of Nations – with or without diplomacy by conference – was retained. It was not until decades later, during the last quarter of the century, that the idea of the concert of Europe faded and was finally thrown out by the nationalists of all countries. Only then did the old system degenerate into anarchy and produce the age of the great wars of this century. After the end of the third great war, the Cold War, we have reason to ask whether another great alliance will be allowed to crumble. Do we want our countries to return to the old system of case-by-case alliances? Are we going to surrender the idea of a perpetual community of the nations of Europe and North America?

21

In Eastern Europe, long-standing accounts between nations are being settled with such anger, venom and blood that new debts are added to the old ones. Western Europe certainly need not fear similar events, but traditional alliances have loosened unexpectedly. A re-nationalisation of Western European politics can be discerned. From the very moment when the Wall in Berlin was breached, political elites in Europe began to worry about united Germany's potential strength. Forty years of close cooperation with Germany in the Atlantic Alliance and the European Community did not prove enough to lay to rest the memories of the world wars. Soon, it was believed, the unified Germans, suddenly comprising 80 million people in a single country, would try to dominate Europe. They would use their central location and power to exploit Eastern Europe's weaknesses; or they would play East and West off against each other; or they might foster a privileged relationship with Russia to the detriment of the West.

So the 'German Question', which until then had been the problem of German partition, reappeared in a new and totally different form. It stimulated President Mitterand to visit President Gorbachev in Kiev in December 1989 to try to persuade him to stall German unification. British Prime Minister Margaret Thatcher, more persuasively, attempted to re-activate residual allied four-power privileges in Berlin in order to slow down the process. The Polish President, General Jaruzelski, thought it appropriate to suggest that Polish troops should also be stationed on German territory. All this occurred while Chancellor Kohl, with the support of all major parties in the German parliament, was emphasising the need for further European integration, for Germany to stay in the western alliance and for NATO to keep its integrated structures including the presence of allied troops on German soil. In these critical early months of 1990 only the American and Canadian governments unconditionally supported the process of unification and even enlisted the support of Soviet Foreign Minister Shevardnadze and Gorbachev.

Chancellor Kohl's pledge to the West helped to bring the 'two-plus-four' talks to a happy end, but did not calm concerns for long. When the Maastricht treaty was debated in France before the referendum in the autumn of 1992, one camp argued in favour of the treaty because it would help to control unified Germany within European structures. In contrast, the opposing camp condemned Maastricht as a German scheme to bring all of Europe into German hands. Both agreed that the Germans needed to be kept under control.

New suspicions of German intentions rose in London and Paris when Yugoslavia began breaking up. Historians will eventually establish to what extent errors of judgement by western Governments contributed to the horrors of the war in Yugoslavia and why the West failed to suppress it in its early stages. The war has so far not only destroyed the cities and villages of Bosnia; it shamed and continues to shame Western governments. It strikes at their capacity for deterring an aggressor, and it destroys western credibility, the very basis for diplomatic crisis management. In the past Nato had managed to deter a superpower. Now it could not even suppress low-level warfare and the re-drawing of territorial borderlines by fourth-rate forces.

Even inside the alliance, NATO's credibility has suffered. How are voters now to be persuaded of the importance of maintaining NATO and the European Union when they see the horrors of war on television each night in their own living rooms, apparently without end? The spectacle undermines NATO's political morale.

Why has Western conflict management failed in the Balkans? There has been a lack of comprehensive and timely analysis of Yugoslavia's domestic situation. Superficially, it seemed that comparisons could be drawn with Northern Ireland or with Basque and Corsican separatism, in which case the threatened state should be maintained. But other considerations seem to have been more important. When war began, the governments in London and Paris sought the advice of older people who remembered the days when the Serbs were on 'our side' and the Croats on the side of the central powers and later became 'Ustaçi-fascists'. They saw the conflict through the lenses of the World Wars and not from the perspective of the Balkan peoples. German demands to have Slovenia and Croatia quickly recognised by the member states of the European Community only seemed to prove that Germany keenly sought the dissolution of Yugoslavia to establish a base for political and economic dominance.

In actual fact, German Foreign Minister Genscher did not move by his own free will but under domestic pressure. It was German public opinion which wanted the fighting to be stopped at once. Early recognition of the principle of national self-determination seemed suitable for the sending of a message to Belgrade: stop fighting, the matter is settled, you cannot change it. But the signal, when eventually sent, was not sufficient. Genscher succeeded in pushing recognition through the Council of Ministers, but his success proved a Pyrrhic victory. Whatever may have been the merits of the argument for early recognition, from this point on Bonn was paralysed. It could not risk further fuelling the suspicion that Germany had interests in the Balkans.

I dwell on these events at such length in order to make a point: it was, to a very large extent, the pre-occupation of European politicians with the 'German Question' which decisively contributed to Western misperceptions of the autonomous causes and forces in former Yugoslavia. One can predict more such unhappy events if political elites in Western Europe do not put aside their preconceived views about each other. These contribute to an engrained fear that history is going to repeat itself. There is a danger of drawing the wrong 'lessons from history' and doing something about it – with yesterday's means. This is more likely to bring about exactly what it was intended to prevent.

Let us look for a moment at two such traditional misconceptions. One is to view our countries as having special 'historical roles'. Is international policy a kind of play, and are nations 'actors' on the 'international stage' playing parts according to a script? Is it, for example, the pre-ordained role of Great Britain to be the arbiter of Europe? Is it equally Germany's role to represent the trouble-maker? Can Germany, because of her geographic position, not do otherwise than de-stabilise Europe? Or is it now, as many Germans have come to believe, the role of others to carry out warfare, while it is the duty of their own country to be a model of morality with a mission to preach peace without force?

Contemporary German pacifism as well as the re-discovery of a 'new German question' are obviously both responses by nations to the World Wars. All the European countries that participated in the great wars have suffered their particular trauma. These wounds had been kept cool for a long time with the icepacks of the Cold War, but they have not yet healed. The First World War proves itself over and over again to be the 'arch-catastrophe' of the twentieth century, as George Kennan observed in his book the *Decline of Bismarck's Order*. All European powers contributed to that catastrophe to varying degrees. All had, with their own imperialism and chauvinism, helped to de-stabilise the system. But Germany, with its restlessness and indiscriminate activism, led the volatile pre-War Europe toward its collapse.

Since then – particularly under the impact of a very effective

British war propaganda – it has become a widely accepted view in Europe that Bismarck's unification of Germany was a mistake and Germany, because of its central location, and weight was too 'heavy' for the balance of the continent – the proverbial loose cannon. But few people take into account the fact that it takes two conditions to make a central geopolitical position volatile: there must be not only irresponsibility in the middle but also instability at the periphery.

There is no scale to determine at which point a country's population, territory or national gross product becomes 'overweight' and bound to destroy the balance. Britain, by far the most powerful state in Europe between the Napoleonic wars and the turn of the century, was never 'too heavy' for the European balance of power. Has the demise of the Soviet Union rendered the United States now 'too heavy' for the global balance of power? If size and economic strength and geopolitical situation influence a state's foreign policy, they only set the parameters, not the intentions and will. Strength and location should not be judged mechanistically, which is to say fatalistically. 'Balance', and more particularly the 'balance of power', is a useful metaphor, but it must not be strained. It applies to free-wheeling masses, not to integral structures.

Similarly, Germany's 'centrality' is a geographical fact but not necessarily a fatal flaw. Germany's central position has existed over centuries without posing inherent dangers. The central position was largely at Austria's disposal without Habsburg emperors developing a particular passion for power or militaristic traditions. Often the opposite was the case, with emperors pursuing a 'cautious' policy. Metternich used Austria's centrality for the moderation of European powers; during the Crimean War Vienna and Berlin used their central position to constrain the conflict between Russia and the two Western powers over the estate of the 'sick man on the Bosphorus'.

A place in the geographical middle of Europe does not automatically pose a threat to neighbours, but central powers do have more borders to defend. They must, unlike powers on the periphery or island powers, place considerably greater emphasis on their security, either by physical and material means or by alliance-building. It appeared to be a recurrent feature of European politics from the end of the middle ages onward that any great power at the periphery of the continent aspiring to become the dominant power of Europe (especially Spain and France) had to have a foothold or at least some allies in Europe's centre. The struggle for supremacy in Europe was always also a battle to get a foot in Germany's door.

Powers along Europe's periphery could only become dominant if they got some kind of support from Europe's core. By the same principle, England always needed a major ally in the centre of Europe to check the progress of a dominant power at the wings of the continent. Examples of this can be seen in the conflict between Francis I of France and the Emperor Charles V over Italy, Swedish and French ambitions during the Thirty Years War, the War of the Spanish Succession, the Seven Years War, the French Revolution and Napoleonic Wars, and Russia's intervention in Eastern Europe during the 1848 Revolutions.

After the Second World War the same principle continued to rule the East-West conflict. As long as the Cold War remained undecided both superpowers projected themselves toward the centre of Europe, thereby dividing the continent. Indeed, without the stationing of a large Soviet army in Germany the Soviet Union would not have been able to maintain its control over Eastern Europe for forty years. The Poles, Czechs and Hungarians would have been able to go their own way as early as the 1950s, as Yugoslavia did under Tito. Only when the Soviet Union was no longer able or willing to intervene with force in the centre of Europe, as in 1989, could the people of Eastern Europe obtain their freedom again.

If it is true that powers on the flanks of the continent needed either a physical presence or support from a major power in the middle of Europe in order to determine the order in Europe, the reverse is also true. A power in the centre of Europe cannot alone impose its order on the continent. The central position allows a voice in the matter, but no more. In fact, Bismarck had always considered the central position of Imperial Germany as a danger rather than an advantage. His chief concern was the possibility that France, humiliated and shrunken by the loss in 1870 of Alsace and Lorraine, would find an ally prepared to share a two-front war to revise the Frankfurt Peace Treaty. That concern explains a great deal of Bismarck's special efforts to cultivate Russia. His system, mainly based on the Dual Alliance with Austria-Hungary, the Triple Alliance including Italy and the Re-Insurance Treaty with Russia, was designed to check this danger and to calm the conflict of interest in the Balkans between the Habsburg Empire and Russia.

However, the fact that Bismarck's system had to be constructed so artificially and partly in secret was an implicit recognition that the 'Concert' of Europe existed no more and that European governments no longer wished to play the tune of moderation. The Congress of Berlin in 1878 was a last vain attempt to bring about a large-scale European settlement in the tradition of Metternich and Castlereagh. It ended with Russia's deep disappointment at having been prevented by Germany from expanding into the Balkans. That resentment was to become one of the sources of future trouble.

After Bismarck's departure in 1890 the European system was characterised by two features. The first was Germany's concern about a Franco-Russian alliance and the danger of a two-front war. Both France and Russia were revisionist powers. Germany's answer was the reinforcement of the Dual Alliance with Austria and the Triple Alliance with Italy, hoping to win over England as well. In that respect, German calculations were defensive and appropriate.

The second feature was England's unwillingness to enter into the firm commitment which the Germans thought necessary. Such a step would also have called for a continuation of England's protective policy in favour of Turkey and Austria in the Balkans. Such a commitment would, however, have gone against the reluctance of the British Liberals and the British public to tie themselves to the continent, not to mention other opinion in Great Britain which felt it necessary to 'restrain' Germany.

German policy after Bismarck committed two major mistakes. The first was to believe that sooner or later England would have to adjust to an alliance with Germany and that German diplomacy could afford to accept nothing short of a formal alliance. The second was to insist that Germany, after her rapid rise to become the major industrial power on the continent, 'owed' it to her new rank as a great power to pursue imperialist interests overseas. These mixed considerations of being threatened on the one hand and of desiring a 'world policy' on the other led to the decision to teach Britain the value of Germany as an ally by raising Germany's nuisance value, building a German navy and adopting a 'lone wolf' policy, the policy of 'a free hand'.

German naval rearmament was the most serious blunder of all the misjudgments after Bismarck. The navy became immensely popular in Germany and the growing fleet symbolised world power; the very presence of the big ships was regarded as an 'international policy'. In the absence of a clear definition of the interests the navy was to serve, the means quickly justified itself. The naval programme and the excitement, which Admiral Tirpitz consciously encouraged, took on a dynamic of its own.

It may have made some sense to have a navy capable of protecting Germany's own coasts against the French or Russian fleets. It can perhaps even be argued that Germany had to have a fleet of overseas cruisers for the protection of her colonies, even though these were in reality unimportant possessions held for pure prestige. But naval rearmament and the building of a battle fleet became a clear challenge to Britain. Matters were made worse by the domestic naval propaganda, which could not help but take on an anti-British tone. There was open talk of a 'risk fleet': a risk for England. Today it seems beyond comprehension that another generation believed it possible to seek security against France and Russia from Britain, and at the same time to challenge Britain as the leading sea power. What German policy actually achieved was to drive Britain into the anti-German camp.

It is not necessary to trace all movements of the European governments in the conflict-laden pre-war era to bring out the point that all the powers contributed significantly, in one way or another, to the collapse of the European 'system' at the end of the century. The idea of moderation was lost. All nations had adopted the credo of robust egotism. All entertained exaggerated ideas of their 'national interests'. All major countries were ruled by the notion that one's own nation was the supreme value. Even international trade was understood as a competition between nations rather than individual companies or branches of industry. Even the smaller European nations contributed by their colonial ambitions to the degeneration of the European order into a Hobbesian society of states, each utterly frightened of the others, but regarded in turn as a predatory wolf by its neighbours.

The error of German policy lay not in the creation of the Second Empire of 1871 nor in being too heavy a mass in the centre of the continent, but in the failure to define German national interests correctly. The security and trade interests of the new industrial power in its precarious central position would have called for the maintenance of the European balance and of open markets. Both interests would have required steady coordination with England, but not necessarily a formal security alliance. Even the few colonies that Germany had, and which were used to justify the naval armament, could have been better secured with the help of the Royal Navy than against it.

In short, German policy after Bismarck failed to understand clearly the vulnerability of Germany's geopolitical situation as a central power without a strong outside ally. The ends of German policy contradicted each other and the means did not even correspond to those ends. Germany wanted to be recognised as a world power, but there was no grand design. To speak of Germany's 'Griff nach der Weltmacht' (Fritz Fischer) is over-interpreting the evidence, particularly evidence of wartime projects rather than pre-war planning. That there was a passion for winning international prestige without a real plan explains to a large extent the bouts of haphazard German activism. A country which cannot define its interests properly and set its policies accordingly will be regarded by others as unpredictable and if, in addition, that country is powerful, as dangerous.

I need not speak here about the Second World War. It followed from the political and moral devastation of the First World War; there cannot be much argument about the causes.

What lesson can be drawn from that unhappy story? First of all, it was a unique situation. What had happened was neither pre-dermined by the central geographical position, nor by the mere size of Germany, nor by German history or the national character in general. The Russian and French roles in the genesis of the First World War are often overlooked. Allied propaganda during the war of course painted friend and foe in white and black. The images stuck.

There is little cause to fear that Germany will again be plagued by great power ambitions. In this respect the lesson of two world wars has been fully understood, indeed to such a degree as to give cause for opposite concerns. 'From being obsessed with power to being oblivious of it', is how Hans-Peter Schwarz has described the turnabout in foreign policy thinking in some sections of German public opinion. It swelled the ranks of the peace movement in the 1970s and destroyed the consensus among German Social Democrats over nuclear deterrence. It broke Helmut Schmidt's government. It showed up again in a conspicous lack of support for the British in the Falklands War and, initially, in the Gulf War and 'out-of-area' operations.

It is, however, reassuring that there is no dispute about either the continued membership of Germany in NATO or the presence of allied troops in Germany. It is true that within NATO and the European Union there is a need for balance, for moderation of the stronger and for consideration of the weaker partners. But the spirit of the team will be damaged if one particular member of the community is placed under suspicion by others and kept in a kind of moral quarantine while her cooperation is nevertheless desired, needed and accepted. One does not have to be a psychologist to understand that this is unwise and offensive and in the end will harm everbody.

Margaret Thatcher has professed with frankness in her memoirs her belief in a new balance of power policy directed against Germany. In other Western European countries too, large sections of the 'political class' are impatiently waiting for signs of renewed German 'assertiveness' and brutality so that they can take timely precautions. Proof of that kind of suspicion was provided during some hectic days in September 1992 at a time of international currency speculation against the franc, the lira and the pound, when some people regarded the refusal of the Bundesbank to lower the German interest rate as German 'muscle flexing' or even a plot by power-hungry Germans against the currencies of their neighbours. Another example concerns the assaults by German skinheads against Turkish workers' housing; there were attempts to explain the ugly incidents not by a close look at their actual causes, but as new examples of an incorrigible leaning of Germans toward violence, racism and Nazism. There were others, however, who noted that similar incidents of hooliganism, xenophobic violence and a growing resentment against a seemingly uncontrolled, massive influx of illegal immigrants and asylum-seekers from the poorest countries of the world were occurring in other countries as well.

The Federal Republic of Germany has opted for the West and wants to stay there, in spite of a very pressing need to devote attention and resources to the reconstruction of the former East Germany and to assist the states of Eastern Europe. Other governments' help is very welcome. The most sensible answer to 'the new German Question' – if it is felt to be such – would be to continue with European cooperation wherever possible. Good sense would demand that three countries in particular, Britain, France and Germany, form a close and equable relationship and resist bouts of national jealousy. This would mean an end to deliberate efforts to have special relationships with one partner to the exclusion of others, such as a British special relationship with the United States at the expense of the continental powers, an Anglo-French Entente at the expense of the Germans, or a Franco-German friendship at the expense of the 'Anglo-Saxons'.

There is also a need for the Germans to come to terms with their own nation. Europe is the community, but nations will continue to provide the emotional homes for national culture, loyalty, sacrifice and identity. Germans feel tempted to negate their nationhood in a vain attempt to flee from the shame which Hitler and his followers brought upon their country. It cannot be easy to live with such a past. But those who want to forget in fact feel ashamed and do remember in a round-about way. And those who try to run away from their nationality into a 'European' identity remember too, in a different manner. No attempt at flight will help. Germany will have to become a 'normal' nation among other nations, in spite of the heavy legacy left by Hitler's twelve years. The process of healing the national conscience demands that proper distinctions be made on all sides between contemplating the past and planning the future. Germans will have to develop a clear idea of German national interests and of appropriate means to pursue them. A bad collective national conscience will not serve as a guide.

What should be Germany's guiding principles? First of all, Germany needs to act in common with partners in NATO and in the European Union. To cooperate as a team is, in addition, a matter of common sense in terms of cost effectiveness and European leverage in the world. Germans will find it easier to adjust realistically to challenges from 'out of area' if they can do so in company with allies. Germany cannot act alone any more, to act together with allies is the only way to avoid eyebrows being raised in Europe. Only when in unison with allies will its actions be regarded as politically 'innocent'. Acting together is the only practical way to lay the ghosts and nightmares of the past, both among Germans and among their neighbours. For Germany it is therefore absolutely vital to keep NATO and the European Union going as viable enterprises; Germany needs both organisations more than other western countries in order to legitimise its actions. A loose organisation like CSCE clearly cannot fulfil such a role.

Any reliable foreign policy needs a definition of national interests. Identifiable national interests are the basis of continuity, credibility and trust. But in a country where nationalism is so utterly discredited as it is in Germany, it is difficult to claim 'national interests' and to distinguish between the nation and nationalism. For the guilt-ridden collective national conscience, the term 'national interest' is banned from the domestic debate and and widely regarded as 'politically incorrect' language. Yet a nation which is not able to talk about its national interests openly and clearly will appear to pursue a hidden, and perhaps suspect, agenda. Cooperating with allies as a matter of principle will help to demonstrate that there is nothing to hide and nothing wrong with having and talking of legitimate German national interests.

The first of these interests is security. From that follows the need to project peace and stability into areas of prospective danger. Presently and for the nearer future this refers mainly to Eastern Europe and to the Moslem countries from Morocco to the Arabian peninsula, and to some selected regions on the southern borders of Russia. Then there is the choice of allies and political means. NATO and the European Community will both have to be understood as and transformed into security organisations in the broad sense of all articles of the Nato treaty, as political and economic communities. But it will not be possible to persuade Americans and Canadians to link their physical security with that of Europe unless Europe remains open to North American goods and services.

Everything else, no matter how desirable, should rank behind these objectives; including for example Germany's institutionalised relations with France and the special relationship with Israel, progress to a political union beyond Maastricht and the creation of a special 'European' defence organisation by reviving the WEU. If there is a French desire to push the Americans out of Europe or to diminish American leadership in the alliance, German national interests call for unambiguous opposition to such schemes.

American leadership is important, and not only for any action 'out of area'. American leadership is also necessary for Nato's internal coordination. Obviously none of the major European countries is ready to appoint one among themselves to be leader of the group, yet there must be leadership. As long as the major European governments do not instinctively assume that Europe belongs together and can act effectively only if it acts together, the European orchestra, especially the players of the wind instruments, will need an American conductor. The American president is the natural chairman of the North Atlantic Commonwealth. He is the only one all the others can accept without major reservations – provided there is a President in the White House who understands that it as a prime American national interest to have Europe as his ally in world affairs.

Germany has, like America, Britain, France and the other members of the European Union, a general national interest in peaceful international relations governed by rules of international law, preventive crisis management, arms control and effective international institutions. It requires that Germany should support the UN. It is not important that Germany win a permanent seat in the UN Security Council and German interests do not call for a spectacular position in the UN; all necessary German influence in the UN can be exercised with the help of allies. As long as long as the UN needs German support, particularly the large German contribution to the United Nations budget, Germany can exert some influence over the dealings of the UN.

A German attempt to obtain formal equality with the five veto powers in the Security Council might even damage German interests. Germany can become a permanent member of the Security Council only if other states from Asia, Latin America and Africa could join as permanent members as well. The most likely result of this change would be to weaken the leadership role of the Security Council and ultimately of the UN as a whole, which is not in the German national interest. It seems to be far better to leave the composition of the Security Council unchanged and meanwhile urge Britain and France to use their privileged position in the UN to voice the views of Europe.

Canning's system – 'every nation for itself' – will not do any more. What is the 'old European system' anyway? If we go only a little further back in the history of our continent, we may well discover that the 'new system' of Castlereagh and Metternich and our own multilateral organisations are simply modern forms of the older notions of the diversity and the unity of Europe.

GREGOR SCHÖLLGEN

National Interest and International Responsibility: Germany's Role in World Affairs[1]

Germany is back. The dramatic developments which took place on the world stage in the late 1980s have led to something which, for almost fifty years, hardly anyone believed would ever happen. The Germans are once again living in a nation-state. They are clearly not finding this easy, mainly because they, of all people, were unprepared for the reunification of their country: uncertainty has become apparent in both the political and the public debates over such issues as the deployment of German soldiers, Germany's role in the United Nations, and the problems posed by refugees and asylum-seekers. This has raised doubts about the ability of the Germans to cope with their new position in world affairs.

Any definition of Germany's new international role must be approached in three steps. First, we shall undertake a brief historical survey; second, we shall take stock of the new situation; and third, we will try to draw some conclusions from this review of the past and the present about the future of Germany's foreign and security policy.

I

One of the striking features of recent European history is that the Germans have always aspired to live in a nation-state precisely when this was least likely to be achievable, for example in the first half of the nineteenth century, and the second half of the twentieth century. The (re)unification of the Germans in a common nation-state was the declared aim of the Federal Republic after 1945, and remained so even when it became clear that this goal was highly unlikely to be realised, particularly from 13 August 1961 when the threatened division of Germany became a reality set in concrete.

The 'nation' was interpreted entirely in terms of the nineteenth-century tradition of a community of Germans, who were linked by a common destiny expressed by their origins, their common linguistic, cultural, economic and political ties, and naturally, their recent history. The point of reference continued to be the German Reich which, according to a judgement handed down by the Federal Constitutional Court in July 1973, had ceased to exist neither at the surrender in 1945 nor at any time subsequently but which, since 1945, had been incapable of acting independently. The idea of the 'German nation' had a great impact on political thinking in Germany, even after the turning points of 1945 and 1949. The strength of the idea is shown by the fact that it remained in the GDR constitution until October 1974, twenty-five years after the foundation of that state. The stubbornness in setting and pursuing this goal is explained largely by the circumstance that throughout their history the Germans have succeeded in living in their own way in a nation-state, the German Reich, only once; and then for the relatively short time-span of seventy-five years.

Twice during this period the German nation-state was given a chance to prove itself. The first opportunity, in the form of the German Kaiserreich founded in 1871, ended in a war of first European, then global dimensions. The second chance was the continued existence of the German Reich beyond the end of this lost war, although in an externally reduced and internally changed form. This second chance ended in a dictatorship, in the catastrophy of a second world war, and in the crime of racially-motivated extermination. None of those involved wanted there to be a third chance.

The foundation of the German nation-state in 1871 was possible only because the European powers permitted it, or had to permit it. It was these powers, plus the USA, which became the crucial shapers of international policy in the twentieth century, and which dissolved the German nation-state seventy-five years after its foundation, after the experience of a second world war. Historically, this was an unprecedented decision. From the point of view of the victors and the erstwhile victims, it was imperative. This insight was based on a dual perception. First, the logic of Germany's political, economic, military and even geographical position meant that a German nation-state would always be a great power and even a possible world power. And, precisely because of this, Germany's security interests were incompatible with those of Europe.

Indeed, from the point of view of its inhabitants, probably the most important condition for the existence of a German nation-state was external strength. To develop, assert, or even re-establish this strength was a major national interest, if not the predominant one. For one thing, those who lived in this state could identify with it only on the condition that this strength existed; this is one of the main reasons why the Weimar Republic, weakened by war, revolution and the 'dictated peace', lacked the support of its citizens and why Adolf Hitler was given a chance. In the German mind, Germany's specific geo-strategic position practically dictated the need for this sort of strength. That this perception was to have devastating consequences does not change the fact that it was widely accepted as obligatory by the Germans of this period.

From the point of view of those who were affected and who had suffered, however, questions of a German nation-state after the second catastrophy allowed only one conclusion, namely, that Germany must never again be permitted to have a national interest and that there must never again be a German great power in the heart of Europe. This meant that any reunification of the two German states after 1945 was out of the question. This attitude could only conceivably change in the wake of a revolution, that is, if the status quo were to be fundamentally overturned. Until the end of the 1980s, however, few thought that this was possible, if only because everyone who wanted to prevent the reappearance on the European scene of a reunited German great power, or even world power, had a vested interest in maintaining the status quo.

In principle, a state which is considered to be a great power because of its social, ethnographical, cultural, economic, political or even geographical significance, or even because of the size of its population, plays a crucial role in determining the destiny of its continent or hemisphere. In a way, Prussia had played this sort of role from 1740 since Frederick the Great seized Silesia. Naturally the German Reich, from its foundation in 1871 under Otto von Bismarck's leadership to the downfall into which Adolf Hitler led it, was a full European great power in this sense, with the exception in some respects, perhaps, of the Weimar years.

As far as their role in world politics was concerned, the Germans had always had a somewhat ambivalent attitude. Certainly in the decades before the outbreak of the First World War, Germany had been a world power. In the age of imperialism, a world power was a great power which participated in the race for colonies, thus acquiring a global significance beyond its own hemisphere and in turn strengthening its position as a great power in its own region. The depth of scepticism among Germany's neighbours, even today, about the brief phase of Germany's colonial policy should actually be quite surprising. Strictly speaking, German 'Weltpolitik' in the age of Bismarck and Wilhelm II hardly differed from the colonial or imperial policy of other European great powers. In fact, compared with those of Britain or France and measured in terms of its successes, Germany's policy was 'ludicrously modest', as the leftist-liberal sociologist Max Weber pointed out in 1916.[2]

The reason for the deep scepticism about this German 'Weltpolitik', which grew over the years and is still noticeable today,[3] is a peculiarity of German political thinking which becomes apparent only in retrospect. During the Wilhelmine period, the Germans were unwilling or perhaps unable to come to terms with an insight that should be a natural part of political thinking in Germany today after unification; as a great power, Germany may not necessarily always be permitted to do what other great powers consider 'normal' for themselves. There are economic, political, geographical and above all, since the 1930s, historical reasons for this.

From the point of view of Germany's neighbours, the Third Reich's policy and Hitler's demand for German 'world domination' fused seamlessly with the actions and ambitions of the Kaiserreich. In declaring himself the advance guard of the popular revisionism of the Weimar period, Hitler seemed immediately to place himself at the head of a movement which wanted to restore the German Reich as a great and world power by cancelling the provisions of the Treaty of Versailles.

Hitler mobilised, exploited and perverted the familiar notions of a German imperial or colonial empire in order to realise his own goals, primarily the racist war of extermination against European Jewry and the creation of 'Lebensraum' for the Germans in east central and eastern Europe. This deception suited many Germans, and for a long time many foreign observers were unaware of it. They saw the campaigns of the Third Reich as merely the most recent expressions of the drive for expansion, starting with the Silesian wars under Frederick the Great and continuing with the annexation of Alsace-Lorraine by Bismarck and with the colonial policy of his successors. Hitler, who sealed the fate of old Prussia, was regarded by his neighbours as its classic representative. They saw the Holocaust as the last, but still typical, form of Prussian-German warfare. The Allied victors of the Second World War simply could not, or did not want to, grasp the fact that the opposite was true: that Hitler had used and perverted the idea of Prussia and the nation-state in order to achieve his real goals, and that he had thus destroyed both Prussia and the nation-state.

Their most urgent concern, therefore, was to prevent the resurgence of Germany as a great power, let alone a world power. The condition for this was to break up the German nation-state, symbolically documented in the formal dissolution of Prussia by the Allies on 25 February 1947. The Allies were unanimous about this aim; by what means it was to be achieved remained disputed. The Cold War was thus among other things an expression of disunity among the victors on the question of how Germany was to be controlled and prevented from rising again. With the end of the Cold War, this control disappeared and the consensus on the main aim fell apart. Fifty years after the Second World War Germany is united again, and is once more on the way to becoming a nation-state, and thus a European great power.

II

The breathtaking upheavals in Europe at the end of the 1860s were unprecedented and unpredictable in form. The tectonic convulsions at the end of the First World War are, however, comparable with the situation today. At that time, three great empires broke apart: Austria-Hungary, the Ottoman Empire and western Russia. The situation today is characterised by the atomisation of another powerful empire, the decline of a mighty military pact, the resurgence of a great power in the centre of the continent and the return of war to Europe. The dramatic events of 1918 had a direct impact on Germany's fate. The German Reich, as the loser of the Great War, was considerably weakened economically, territorially, militarily and as a colonial or world power. But it remained a nation-state and continued to be a viable, stable and significant factor in the heart of Europe. It was still a great power.

Recent developments had a comparable impact. The Germans have been given a third chance; they have again been granted the nation-state status which was considered unattainable, and overnight the Federal Republic has once again been catapulted into the role of a continental great power with global significance. This situation requires the Germans to cope with their new power, and thus calls for a special responsibility. The prerequisite is the realistic, sober and, above all, fully aware recognition that German foreign, security and economic policy, even its policy on asylum-seekers, is power policy.

We can certainly argue about whether Germany should be described as a great power with global significance, and even about how a great power should be defined today. In the first place, Germany's domestic situation since unification hardly encourages it to play an active role as a great power. The enormous problems which the unification process has uncovered at practically all levels – the impact of the recession, the resurgence of xenophobia and anti-Semitism – have made many observers suspect that for the first time in its history the Federal Republic could be a potentially unstable country. This hardly provides an adequate foundation for a great power.

Second, unified Germany possesses neither its own nuclear weapons nor a permanent seat in the UN Security Council. These two criteria defined France's, Britain's and China's status as great powers during the Cold War. Since its end, however, the criteria which define a great power have changed. The dissolution of the Soviet Union immediately brought three new nuclear powers into being, and as more and more countries, especially those in the Third World, approach this threshold the significance of possessing nuclear weapons for the position of a state within the community of nations decreases.

Because the classic status symbols of the Cold War are today playing an increasingly minor political role, the Federal Republic is no longer the medium-sized power, prospering in the lee of the East-West conflict, that it was before re-unification. One reason lies in the history of the German nation-state which was also always a great power, so that the dissolution of the one implied the dismantling of the other. When the status of such a country changes – as is the case with re-unification – this necessarily means more than a correction of figures, data and balances in continental statistics.

To be sure, these are impressive enough in the case of unified Germany. Since re-unification, the Federal Republic has a larger than average population and its territory is considerable. Naturally these factors gain in relative importance as the process of political and territorial atomisation in Southeast and Eastern Europe accelerates through the dissolution of the Soviet Union, Yugoslavia and Czechoslovakia; German re-unification contrasts with the general trend towards political dissolution in Europe. Added to these are a high level of education in the Federal Republic, a comparatively clean environment, and a huge economy which is being further boosted by European integration.

Germany's new importance is demonstrated by its position within the European Community. It is hardly conceivable that any important resolution could be taken against Germany's wishes and, naturally, this reflects Germany's economic dominance in Europe. The Federal Republic has one of the strongest currencies in the world, and certainly the strongest in the continent. The excited reactions to the Bundesbank's interest rate policy and the turbulence, consistently blamed on Germany, which hit the European Monetary System during the French referendum on Maastricht demonstrated this in the autumn of 1992.

Not least, the Federal Republic is anything but a military dwarf. Admittedly it is not a nuclear power, and in 1990 it agreed to reduce the effective strength of the Bundeswehr to 370,000 in acknowledgement of Soviet agreement to German unification, within the framework of the negotiations on conventional force reductions in Europe. In addition, the Bundeswehr's freedom of movement is largely constrained by NATO's integrated command structure, and continuing debates about the future role of the Bundeswehr have an impact. Nonetheless, at a time when the old structures including military ones are disintegrating in eastern Europe, this army in the centre of the Continent, even if it is subject to such limitations, does have considerable weight.

Finally, Germany has two qualities which characterise a great power these days: first it has the capacity to sabotage the functioning of the international system by non-cooperation,[4] and it is a magnet for a potentially huge army of persecuted, starving and homeless people as well as for a growing number of crisis-ridden states in Eastern Europe and beyond. These are related to the factors already mentioned, especially of course to Germany's economic strength and relative prosperity, but also to the dissemination of the German language in Eastern and Central Europe. This attraction also constitutes power and calls for special responsibility from Germany.

The extent to which Germany already finds itself in the role of a continental great power with global political significance becomes clear when we look at the fears and expectations of its neighbours. Some Europeans, the *New York Times* wrote in December 1991, 'cannot shake the suspicion that Germany has simply adopted new tactics to pursue its earlier goal of continental hegemony'.[5] This is by no means an isolated voice; on the contrary, the comparison between unified Germany and the German Reich, especially the Third Reich, is highly fashionable, particularly among Germany's western neighbours and allies.[6]

With good reason, these latter had made sure that the old Federal Republic, with only limited sovereignty, was firmly integrated into international organisations. Starting as early as 1950 with the European Coal and Steel Community, these included the European Community and NATO as well as to a certain extent the CSCE and the UN. Of course this integration was fully in accord with German interests, for all these organisations offered and still offer the Federal Republic opportunities for development of various sorts, as well as external security. Moreover, taken together, they provided an outer framework without which the unification of Germany would have been difficult to imagine. They gave Germany's neighbours some guarantee that a unified Germany would not fall back into the old mistake of pursuing isolated great power, or even world power, politics. A number of Germany's western neighbours still see potential dangers lurking here, however, as the revival of old clichés, prejudices, and stereotypes of the enemy demonstrates.

The views of the young German nation-state held by the states of Eastern, Southeastern, and East Central Europe offer a highly charged contrast. These countries have enormous expectations of the new great power in the heart of Europe, which at least from the outside looks stable. It is remarkable that they are prepared, indeed, determined to no longer see the future – at least primarily – in terms of the past; in other words, in terms of two world wars and, above all, the Third Reich's racist extermination campaign. But the decline of the Soviet Union and the dissolution of the unifying myth of the 'great patriotic war' went hand in hand. Thus it seems for the people of these countries, and especially for the post-war generations who did not experience the German war of extermination at first hand, that its horrors seem to have faded in relation to the hated communist and Stalinist dictatorships, into which they were born and under which they had to suffer until the end of the 1980s.

It is not surprising that Germany's western neighbours have registered – with occasional alarm – this growing interest by the states of eastern Europe and especially Russia in the new German great power. This has much to do with the enormous significance of the process of upheaval and its impact on the fate of the entire Continent. The fact that Russian leaders are approaching Germany with requests for support and cooperation, reminds some sceptical observers of the German-Soviet cooperation of the inter-war period. This began with Rapallo, but is naturally always interpreted from the perspective of its end, the Hitler-Stalin Pact. The fear that Russia and Germany could come to an agreement at the expense of others, as in the inter-war period increases as, with the end of the Cold War, the time-tested order develops cracks. Not only are a number of supra-national organisations such as NATO, the CSCE, and the UN, in which the Federal Republic is firmly anchored, going through a process of transformation whose outcome is uncertain, but the chances of European political integration in federal form seem to be dwindling.

Today it seems that, despite all resolutions, announcements and pleas, political union in the original and real sense is unlikely to become a reality in the foreseeable future. The prospect that the failure of political union could permanently set back the process of European integration also in those aras which most require progress – economic policy, security policy, refugee policy and environmental policy – is serious. Above all, we cannot exclude the possibility that the failure of European integration in these areas might lead to a resurgence of nationalism in Western Europe. Nobody will desire this, however, because an explosive combination with the nationalisms of Eastern and Southeastern Europe cannot in principle be excluded. A look at the first half of this century shows us the possible results.

Europe, including the western part of the continent, is balanced on a knife-edge. It will be necessary to prevent any renewed flaring up of nationalism, while giving the revival of the national idea the space which it obviously needs in order to be able to develop in a healthy direction. Events since the end of the 1980s have made it clear that despite, or perhaps because of, attempts to achieve European integration, the idea of the nation-state has not disappeared. It obviously cannot simply be swept away; on the contrary, as John Major has recently pointed out: 'For us, the nation state is here to stay.'[7] Indeed it is difficult to imagine that Basques, Walloons, or Irish will believe that the national idea is dead. And why should they, as the German example has clearly demonstrated that the (re)construction of a nation state in Europe is possible even in an apparently hopeless case? After all, German unification in itself is an example for a general trend in Europe since the late 1980s, the trend towards re-nationalisation of the old continent.

III

At a time when, in many countries, people are just beginning to get used to the idea of the nation-state once more, perhaps the most important European task is to prevent excesses and to stop this idea from turning into nationalism or chauvinism once again. This applies especially to Germany. No other country in western Europe bid farewell to the idea of a united nation-state so thoroughly and so definitely as did Germany, which was divided for almost half a century.

Therefore in no other comparable case is it so difficult to develop a healthy relationship with the nation-state, which in any case the Germans have experienced for only about seventy-five years. In addition, some of the responsibilities of the nation-state have already been delegated to the European or Atlantic communities. A further factor is the psychological split, which followed the external division of the country. In no other western European country, finally, is the outbreak of xenophobia and anti-Semitism so repellent as in Germany with its history. Nowhere else in the western half of Europe do such outbreaks arouse the fear that individual outbursts could again coalesce into organised violence both at home and abroad.

Nonetheless, to the extent that Europe distances itself from political union again, the Federal Republic must also 'become a normal European nation-state'.[8] For reasons which lie in their country's most recent history, however, the Germans are not prepared for this. How could they be, given that they have lived in a unified nation-state only once, during the German Reich, and that as a result of the catastrophes which this unleashed, they have, over fifty years, become accustomed to the idea of its definitive end? By 1988 there was little opposition to Egon Bahr's statement that anyone who raised the German Question disturbed Europe.[9]

The new situation therefore involves an enormous responsibility. As a reborn nation-state, Germany will have to define its national interests clearly and plainly, both for itself and for others. The Federal Republic has taken a number of steps to prevent these from coming into conflict with the security interests of others again. Thus on several occasions it renounced any territorial claims going beyond the status quo – first as long ago as 1970-73 in the *Ostverträge* and then, since re-unification, in a series of agreements with its eastern neighbours, most notably on 14 November 1990 in the border treaty with Poland. Furthermore, in the preamble to its Basic Law, the Federal Republic has already expressed the will of its citizens 'to promote world peace as an equal member of a united Europe'. This sets an important but also very wide framework.

It seems that a growing number of observers and people involved in Europe are aware that while the integration of the Federal Republic into Europe is, for the moment, an important common interest, it should not take a form which will in the long term inhibit the development of Germany and with it, the development of the Continent. In a completely transformed world, the Federal Republic will have to play a part which matches its importance, by no means for selfish reasons only. Europe needs Germany, and a Germany in the heart of Europe which is too weak is, under existing circumstances, no less worrysome than one which is too strong.

The Federal Republic must therefore define its national interests. This presupposes taking stock of the new situation realistically. We must grasp that Germany has long since been in a position of power. A number of developments have contributed to this situation; the dramatic disintegration of the old power structures of eastern Europe, Germany's own significance in almost all areas, clearly increasing since re-unification, and its power to attract others, especially a rapidly-growing number of suffering people. This rather sober finding implies another; power is a factor in the lives of individuals, peoples and states. For this reason, power contains within itself from the beginning both the danger of abuse and the opportunity to be placed in the service of life-saving, peace-keeping and civilised purposes.

In a world which is under threat of becoming disjointed, the Germans are called upon to make their power available and to use it in the latter, positive, sense. Potential cases are as diverse as the forms in which this power can, or must, be used. They range from humanitarian and economic support to massive intervention, including the use of military means. The Federal Republic, a wealthy European great power which has, for the time being, achieved its aims, can no longer withdraw from what the peace and conflict researcher Dieter Senghaas has called the development of a 'culture of legitimate intervention' which must be directed against 'the excesses of policies which have no respect for human beings'.[10] For the moment, however, there can be no question of German soldiers being deployed in areas where they could directly evoke memories of the war waged by the Third Reich; and, of course, German military action will be possible only within the framework of international action and in accordance with the UN Charter.

The Federal Republic will also have to signal its readiness to take part in collective security measures and even in re-establishing the peace, in order to demonstrate that it is both willing, and if necessary able, to shoulder the contractual responsibilities which arise out of its membership in organisations of collective security or collective self-defence. Germany can see itself one day being in a position to have to appeal to these itself. War and civil war are everyday realities again, even in Europe, and nobody knows where and when the violence will end.

Today, the main task of the Atlantic Alliance, which is adapting to changes in the international situation, is to prepare to avert the dangers which might arise out of unpredictable developments on the closer or more distant periphery of western Europe. Nobody would dismiss as unfounded speculation the possibility of another attempted coup in Russia, with potentially incalculable consequences for European and world security. We are aware of the speech by the Russian foreign minister Kozyrev at the CSCE meeting in December 1992, when he issued a warning about a takeover by 'national-patriotic' forces in Moscow.[11] Nobody can guarantee that crises and wars such as the Gulf War will always be limitable. Nobody dares to predict the virulence and dimensions which the nationalist issue in Eastern, Southeastern, or East Central Europe might assume if it were to become activated or acute outside the former Soviet Union and Yugoslavia. Nobody can exclude the possibility that, in the short or long term, some of the states of Western Europe might be subjected to the threat of blackmail, whether by large-scale disruption of vital oil supplies, or by the threatened use of nuclear weapons which are practically freely available on the world market today. Such threats may be used by particular groups which want to achieve certain political, or religious goals.

The time of calculable deterrence, based on the controlled and controllable nuclear stalemate of the Cold War, is over.[12] North Korea's temporary cancellation of the treaty banning nuclear weapons, whatever its motives, demonstrated this on 12 March 1993. So did the Ukraine's decision of 2 July 1993 formally to assert its ownership of all nuclear weapons on its territory and thereby declare itself a nuclear power.

Expressing an unequivocal attitude towards international organisations of collective self-defence, above all NATO, is an outstanding national interest of the Federal Republic, a non-nuclear power. Its attitude must be formulated in full awareness of the fact that alliances rest on mutuality, and cannot be the subject of opportunist interpretations. Discussions about the alliance such as those which took place during the Gulf War with reference to the NATO partner Turkey are inappropriate. The issue of whether to send a German destroyer to a crisis area on a UN tour of inspection within the framework of a WEU mission and as part of a NATO force must not give rise to a controversy lasting weeks, as happened in the summer of 1992. It was also rather difficult to understand Germany's long deliberations early in 1993 on whether to leave the Bundesluftwaffe crews on board NATO AWACS planes carrying out UN resolutions concerning the protection of the people of Bosnia. It is not easier to understand, at least for many foreign observers, why genuine political decisions on obligations towards the UN, WEU or NATO are being shuffled off onto the constitutional court, as in the case of Germany's participation in UNISOM II.[13]

Thus in declaring its willingness to deploy its political, economic and, if necessary, military power, the Federal Republic must pursue a number of goals. First, as we have seen, it must demonstrate its ability to become part of an alliance. Second, Germany has a vital interest in combating the causes of large-scale population movements – such as systematic genocide, mass expulsions, or the starvation of millions – where this is possible by means of economic or humanitarian aid, and in the most extreme cases, if necessary, by collective military means. Third, Germany must have a genuine interest in exercising its influence over decisions of those international communities to which it belongs. Finally, as one of the most potent states in the world, Germany is able to participate actively in preventing international organisations from momentous setbacks as in Cambodia, Haiti, Somalia or Bosnia; but this is only possible if Germany does not claim a special status (*Sonderrolle*) but rather acts as one nation among others.

In placing its power in the service of this common cause, and in defining this common cause as a national interest – as, under present-day conditions, it is – Germany would convincingly demonstrate that its national interests and the security interests of its neighbours are no longer mutually exclusive. By doing so, the second German nation-state, like the first, would opt for the deployment of its power but against its misuse; it would rather see power as giving Germany a chance to participate in checking crises and wars and in avoiding catastrophes. This is an enormous challenge. In previous similar situations, German policy has always ended in crisis and disaster. The Germans are called upon to accept a responsibility commensurate with the status of their country as a sovereign, equal nation-state and with its strength as a European great power, without repressing, forgetting, or least of all repeating the clumsiness, mistakes and crimes of the first half of this century whose consequences can be felt to the present day. The fate of Europe could to some extent depend on whether Germany passes this test, and on whether the Germans understand that their national interest today consists of shouldering their international responsibilities.

Notes

1. A more detailed discussion of the issues raised in this paper can be found in Gregor Schöllgen, *Angst vor der Macht. Die Deutschen und ihre Außenpolitik*, Berlin and Frankfurt/M., 1993.
2. Max Weber, 'Deutschland unter den europäischen Weltmächten', in Weber, *Gesammelte Politische Schriften*, J. Winckelmann (ed.), 3rd edn., Tübingen, 1971, pp. 157 ff., quotation on p. 160.
3. Raimond Poidevin, *Die unruhige Großmacht. Deutschland und die Welt im 20. Jahrundert*, Freiburg and Würzburg, 1985, is representative of many others.
4. See the definition of 'great power' by Ryohei Murat, 'Die japanische Außenpolitik in den neunziger Jahren', *Europa-Archiv* 48, 1993, p. 578.
5. Stephen Kinzer, 'Germany Is a Challenge for Post-Soviet Europe', *The New York Times*, 27 December 1991.
6. See Gregor Schöllgen, 'Deutschlands neue Lage. Die USA, die Bundesrepublik Deutschland und die Zukunft des westlichen Bündnisses', *Europa-Archiv*, 47, 1992, pp. 125 ff.
7. John Major, 'Raise your eyes, there is a land beyond', *The Economist*, 25 September 1993.

8. Wolf Lepenies, 'Zum Sprechen bringen. Für einen Patriotismus der Intellektuellen', *Frankfurter Allgemeine Zeitung*, 23 October 1992.

9. Egon Bahr, 'Rede über das eigene Land: Deutschland', in Bahr, *Sicherheit für und vor Deutschland. Vom Wandel durch Annäherung zur Europäischen Sicherheitsgemeinschaft*, Munich and Vienna, 1991, p. 141.

10. Dieter Senghaas, 'Weltinnenpolitik - Ansätze für ein Konzept', *Europa-Archiv*, 47, 1992, pp. 643 ff., quotations on pp. 650-2.

11. Andrei Kozyrev, 'The new Russia and the Atlantic Alliance', *NATO-Review*, 1, 1993, pp. 3ff., here p. 4.

12. Gregory L. Schulte, 'NATO's nuclear forces in a changing world', *NATO Review*, 1, 1993, pp. 17 ff.

13. See Gregor Schöllgen, 'Putting Germany's post-unification foreign policy to the test', *NATO Review*, 2, 1993, pp. 15 ff.

JOACHIM FEST

Europe in a Cul-de-sac

Looking back on half a century of attempts at European unification, one sometimes feels as though one were in a museum. The rooms devoted to the early period contain bold sketches. Then come a few finished studies, first efforts at painting, all in broad perspectives. Many believe that the promise of these early works is soon to be realised; only the discerning eye can detect how much these pictures owe to artistic illusion. And then, even before mastery is achieved, there are signs of fatigue and staleness, a loss of creative impulse and of perception. Finally in the last room the images convey nothing more than a sense of strained artifice. The parts no longer make a whole. Instead everything collapses into nightmare scenarios, surreal images in which it is impossible to recognise the original intentions.

Today Europe does indeed seem to be rather like a museum: a world of yesterday's memories, grand visions which no one can quite reconcile with the world as it really is. Now that Europe is coming face-to-face with reality, the approval rates which were once so high are plummeting in all countries. People everywhere fear the loss of their way of life, of their traditions and of their freedom to control their own affairs. No one can allay these fears, not the politicians in Babylonian Brussels, not the European lawyers with their inscrutable jargon or *Volapük* as de Gaulle put it, and least of all the technocrats, who spend their time devising new norms for European apples, for the curvature of European cucumbers, for the size of European condoms, of the condition of animals in European zoos.

To make this worse, no one has the faintest notion of what form Europe should take. From the outset the concept has been encumbered with a hidden contradiction. There were those who

51

aimed at a loose economic association garnished with a few vague political platitudes, and then there were the radical Europeans, who strove for a federal model. Now that these notions are taking on concrete form, the contradiction between them is emerging with great force. Oracular utterances can no longer befog the issue. We do not even know where the frontiers of this notional Union are to be. Do Poland, the Czech and the Slav republics or Hungary belong? Time will solve that problem, say determined Europeans. But time rarely solves anything.

In one of the pictures of that imaginary museum, the founders are portrayed as in old votive paintings: there is the figure of Europe enveloped in Carolingian insignia, with behind her a deep blue background with a crown of stars. At her feet are Winston Churchill, George Marshall, Adenauer and Schuman, as well as Gasperi and Jean Monnet, Hallstein and de Gaulle. But also, set apart yet unmistakeable, there are the princes of the abyss, Adolf Hitler and Josef Stalin.

For it was not only the shock created by Hitler's mutilation of Europe which brought its nations together at the end of the Second World War. Soviet power, which cast its mighty shadow over the remnants of the Eurasian continent, was always the other driving impulse. And whenever in the 1950s and 1960s the hastily constructed machinery began to splutter, as it did after the collapse of the European Defence Community or the Anglo-French Suez fiasco, the ghost of the Soviet dictator reappeared on the stage in the role of the great integrator. Thus the desire for European Union was revived time and time again. This proves once more what the fluctuating history of Europe has taught us since the Middle Ages, that every European rapprochement was only ever the manifestation of an instinct for survival. The power of the idea never reflected anything but the power of the enemy at the gates.

Of course there were other motivating forces at work, but these were always second thoughts, which nobody expressed openly but everyone pursued. Thus for example the German enthusiasm for Europe during the 1950s was conditioned by the need for military protection and for open markets, but above all was driven by the desire to remove the stain of war, crime and defeat. No doubt this enthusiasm was, for the most part, well meant. But it was also rather naive and motivated by the wish to forget the past and its wounds more quickly than was possible for Germany's former enemies.

The Federal Republic was founded under many auspices, not the

least of which was the figure of Konrad Adenauer. By no means naive,
Adenauer used Europe as an instrument to reconcile Germany once
and for all with its neighbours, especially France. For France was the
other nucleus of the European idea, and for a long time it was
accepted as a foregone conclusion that the policy of German-French
rapprochement lay at the heart of the European idea. But Paris was not
without ulterior motives either. France had discovered, not without
pain, that its ambition to be a great power corresponded even less
with reality than it had after the First World War. Seeing the Federal
Republic leap from one *Wunder* to the next, France saw a close
partnership with that country as an opportunity to better its chances
in the club of the truly mighty, in keeping with its unrequited dreams
of national glory. There is no doubt that France took the role of
guardian in this relationship, hoping thereby to throw the increasing
weight of its German ward on its own scales and keep the rest of the
world out of European affairs.

In all French declarations for the European cause, the inclination
to deny other great powers a voice in the decision-making process
has been unmistakeable. From the outset it was President de Gaulle
who recognised France's particular interest in adopting this stance,
for example in his stubborn opposition to Britain's joining the
European Economic Community and in France's withdrawal from
NATO as well as in countless other manoeuvres, vetos and diatribes.
To the great satisfaction of France, British diplomacy in particular
took years to adjust to the fact that its traditional services as referee
on the continent of Europe were no longer required. Britain's
resentful warnings against the 'German threat' and the French
striving for supremacy suddenly went unheeded. The jingoistic press
took up these slogans with relish, and the tabloids vied with each
other in orgies of anti-European sentiment. Even in the late 1960s,
Harold Macmillan conjured up the threat of a continental blockade,
and the 'Economist' wrote that Germany and France had no positive
aims; their harmonious relations depended on nothing other than
mistrust and resentment of England.

The suspicions and ulterior motives of all the three main European
states were deeply rooted in the foundations of that strange entity
which went by the name of 'European Community'. As it gradually
grew, not without strenuous efforts, setbacks and sporadic bursts of
optimism, and developed endless new committees, experts and
procedures with all the requisite bureaucratic termitariums, one
could always say it was moving ahead. But over and above the vapid

preamble of the EEC treaty about the 'ever-closer union of the European peoples', no one could really say how and whither it was moving.

It was not least the ulterior motives harboured by each of them which led the partners to mask their aims with nebulous generalisations. There was lofty talk of union, federation or association, but no one could or would express what these words meant. Charles de Gaulle, who loved carving his intentions in cryptic marble, so to speak, was particularly obscure. What he and all later French diplomacy wanted was very simple: not a *communauté*, but an alliance under French leadership, but that has been lost in the morass of verbiage. In effect, economic integration was the only thing that was promoted. The statesmen soon recognised that only the economy has the flexible irreverence towards the status quo which this monumental task required. Even where they had only just come into being after the war, the political structures formed a system of traditions, venerable authorities and near-sacred institutions which no one could touch.

Convinced Europeans consoled themselves over and over again with the idea that economic integration would sooner or later be followed by political union. But that was and is a simplistic Marxist illusion. Both world wars, indeed all the wars of this century, have repeatedly shown how quickly the mesh of economic co-operation is torn asunder by political conflict. Common Market and separate statehood are basically the norm. The Rome Treaties establishing the European Economic Community therefore contained many clauses which secured the right of each state to act alone on the international stage and pay no attention to interference by other powers. There was talk of the *finalité politique* but at this stage such words did not yet have a price.

All the same, blind confidence in the political dynamics of economic union persisted: this was the much-evoked 'logic of fact', a phrase which was dredged up in innumerable speeches on Europe, although the facts spoke against it and it was impossible to detect any logic there either. The consequences were inevitable. As always when a vision falls into the mill-wheels of political routine, the substance was ground to dust.

But it was not this alone which shattered the initial enthusiasm; in addition, Europe soon committed a deadly sin against the spirit of its own idea when Gaullist France forced the common agricultural policy out of the member countries. In fact, the policy was the opposite of a market; it was an area of price guarantees, quotas, premiums and subsidies. It was also not 'common', since every national ministry had to justify the compromises it had wrangled over to its own people. The 'Green Front', as the European agricultural lobby was soon dubbed because of its massive interventions backed up by strikes and road blockades, not only became the focus of all European crises since the seventies but also discredited the entire concept. Public outrage was powerless in the face of repeated struggles over quotas and compensations, and was equally powerless against the absurdity of butter mountains and milk lakes and the whole inscrutable system of expensive follies devised by a bureaucracy which was expanding at a frightening pace. It satisfied no one and enraged everyone. But the development continued undaunted and, because it was not what people had envisaged, Europe eventually became indifferent. The vision began to fade.

Nevertheless there was one area in which Europe had been successful. Although none of the political aims had been achieved and integration, whatever it meant, had not progressed an inch, the Community had brought about the internal market of the twelve EC member states, which neared completion at the end of the 1980s. Since everyone benefited from it, the internal market bore its meaning and its justification in itself. This, however, was only one success amid several failures. Convinced Europeans may have felt betrayed by the course of events, but they had learnt long since to submit to the pressure of circumstances and live with delaying tactics.

The idea of European Union suddenly received a new and unexpected thrust when the Soviet Union began to disintegrate in the autumn of 1989. The European idea had always rested on the premise of a divided world; the experiences and worries of the 1950s had carried the concept forward to the threshold of the 1990s. Now everything changed at once. It was no longer pressure from outside which advanced the cause; pressure now came also from within, from the dreaded united Germany which was already beginning to haunt some dreams in the shape of a 'Fourth Reich'. France's worries also came into play; finding herself abruptly forced onto the periphery, France realised that she could only assume the leading role she coveted so much in a more closely-knit Europe.

Suddenly the pressure was on. The hectic events between 1990 and 1992 set in motion the somewhat rusty European wheels which had ground to a near halt in the quagmire of Brussels routine. The aim now was to clamp the community together quickly and tightly and to create irrevocable ties. It was no longer the great internal market, with the famous four freedoms of circulation, peoples, goods and services, which was to be effected on schedule; monetary union with a common central bank as its keeper was also planned with a fixed deadline. At the same time the first steps were to be taken towards political union with a common foreign policy and a common defence policy. But at this point opposition was met and there was a hasty retreat to the perfunctory.

The wording on which the heads of government finally agreed shows the extent to which they got lost in verbiage. Every single word was the result of tough bargaining and the price was that the final words were almost entirely devoid of meaning: 'The common foreign and defence policy shall include all questions related to the security of the Union, including the eventual framing of a common defence policy, which might in time lead to a common defence.' Three political principles were formulated: closeness to the people, the safeguarding of national identities and subsidiarity. But these were three words or phrases which had little meaning and really only confirmed the deficiencies of Europe in the eyes of the public.

The term for this combination of fuss, bustle and empty phrases is 'Maastricht'. The passage quoted is listed as article J 4 point 1 in the Maastricht Treaty. For all the emphatic words with which the treaty was extolled by the powers that be as a 'historic event', the public echo was astonishingly small. The event met with the same reaction that all things European had elicited for years; it was simply greeted with the weary applause of the professional Euro-claque, while the people swallowed it more or less indifferently.

At this point the veil of big words and self-serving routine tore apart. In a referendum on 2 June 1992, the Danes voted against the treaty, albeit with a small majority. The surprise could not have been greater. Suddenly everything was up in the air, for according to its own wording the treaty was to come into effect 'provided that all the ratification documents had been deposited'. Danish ratification would now be lacking. Amid general speculation about the motives for the rejection it was felt that the government in Copenhagen had made a terrible mistake. For in order to inform the public, the Danish government had distributed millions of copies of the Treaty of European Union together with the final agreement of the Maastricht conference, the appended supplementary protocols, the Foundation Treaty of the European Community in the version of the Treaty of the European Union, the Single European Act, the agreements on common institutions and on the establishment of the Council and the Commission and the Act on the Introduction of European Elections – altogether a document in which every text contained another, like the famous Russian doll. Including the seventeen supplements and the thirty-three appended declarations the document not only amounted to about 250 pages, but it was also littered with cross references, revocations and amendments, a Galimatias of legalistic bureaucratic obsession. In this thicket no one was able to make out what Europe was and should be. The Danish Foreign Minister described the suspicions expressed in the result of the Danish referendum fairly accurately when he adapted a phrase from a princely compatriot: 'To be or not to be: that is the answer'.

The European governments, like the civil servants and politicans in Brussels and Strasburg, all tried to ignore the outcome of the referendum as if by arrangement. They may well have succeeded, had the French president not decided shortly beforehand, in one of those tactical manoeuvres on which he prides himself, to use the European issue as a vehicle for a vote of confidence in his own government. In the event Mitterrand's opponents at home felt encouraged by the outcome of the Danish Referendum to condemn Europe if need be, and the treaties gave the President no cover. A state of emergency ensued. For the first time since the failed European Defence Community of 1954 there arose a dispute in which Europe and the consequences of its union were debated with impassioned gravity. Nebulous visions, which had provided such convenient hiding places, were no longer the issue; concrete restrictions and renunciations of sovereignty were now under discussion. At this point the reservations which had from the outset been buried deep in the foundations of the Community came to the fore. These now rocked the whole edifice.

Above it all it became clear how little the trauma of German power had healed. At times it seemed as though France was not fighting over the Maastricht Treaty, but, as Alfred Grosser wrote, over the most suitable means of locking her neighbour beyond the Rhine in a cage. Re-unification had revived all the latent fears, and then in the midst of the French debate the Rostock riots broke out. Molotov cocktails were thrown into a home for asylum seekers. It was as though the Germans themselves had wanted to provide proof that the 'old demons' had reawakened. Europe is afraid of the uncontrollable German 'totalitarian tendency'; that was the message

of innumerable speeches, comments and talkshows. Deep in the
German 'soul', it was believed, there lay a combination of
'irrationalism and frightening strength'. The only reason the
Germans were interested in Europe was to turn the defeat of 1945
into victory and the subjugation of its neighbours: a well-known
French publicist wrote, 'the shadow of "Faust" darkens the old
continent again'.

However, these worries provided both sides with arguments. The
opponents of Union used the fear of the Germans to warn against
'national suicide', while advocates claimed that Maastricht was
Europe's answer to re-unification and would serve as a sort of sign
of the cross to preserve the Germans from their 'evil spirits'. One
French newspaper spelt out more blatantly than anyone else and
without any literary trimmings what France expected from monetary
union; in an article headlined 'From Versailles to Maastricht', the
paper said: 'In the twenties one used to say "Germany will pay". It
pays today: Maastricht is the Treaty of Versailles without war.'

It was brought strongly home through this debate just how remote
Europe (and everything that was ever meant by that word) still was.
Now all the great avowals and accolades over war graves seemed like
sentimental *mises en scène*, behind which the most ancient phantoms
were still at work. Incessant talk about the return of 'German
demons' only revealed how tightly the French were in the grip of their
own demons, as if time had stood still. But it was not only the French;
the abysses of the past opened up all over Europe, with the loudest
fears coming from Britain and Italy. And yet again events gave them
a pretext; this time it was the high interest rate policy of the
Bundesbank. Only then did it dawn on those involved what they had
agreed to in Maastricht. The Bundesbank had precisely that
independence in the face of a wasteful or lax fiscal policy with which
the Central European Bank was to be equipped according to the
Maastricht Treaty, but at the same time the heads of state realised
that monetary union required a uniform economic policy. That in
turn meant having to give up monetary sovereignty, and none of the
participants was willing to do so. François Mitterand openly stated
that the Central European Bank would be independent in name but
not in fact.

Maastricht was not a departure to new shores, despite all the
rhetoric, but rather, as one French observer said, 'only a calculated
move against the predominance of the Bundesbank and against the
existence of an independent German currency'. Another outspoken

commentator, whom we have to thank for various candid words, put it even more bluntly: 'It is the foremost aim of the Treaty to get rid of the German mark.'

In addition, the economic and political, but above all the psychological preparation for the Treaty was totally inadequate. To put it mildly, too much was given over to a self-fulfilling European dynamic. Although the Brussels administration had patiently undermined national competences over the years, nothing had taken their place. Above all, there was not even the outline of a common European consciousness, nor had the European interest been defined. In the face of a completely changed international situation, all that was left was 'yesterday's answers to yesterday's problems', as Margaret Thatcher triumphantly scoffed. No constitutional debate came about nor did a decision on 'deepening' or 'enlargement'; in short there was nothing to establish the concept of Europe in the minds or hearts of the people. Europe remained a mere 'company nameplate' (Herbert Lüthy), behind which the old vanities of nation-states continued to live as silent ghosts.

Not even the nameplate kept what it promised. The many opt-outs which Britain, Portugal and Denmark pushed through were nothing if not anticipated or extorted breaches of contract. The predictable inability of some of the states to meet the criteria of convergence and monetary union demonstrate what is repeatedly denied: that there will be a Europe of different speeds. The Treaties remain as silent on this as they are on the contradictions between a national finance policy and a supra-national currency policy, between a partially realised federal state and a confederation of states, between open frontiers and internal security. It looks as though these and many other uncertainties have simply been ignored under the pressure of the political chanceries. But people sense how incomplete the building is in which they are supposed to feel at home, how many dark niches, unknown siderooms and even trap doors it contains.

Not without cause, governments now think that all European populations would reject the Treaty if they were to hold a referendum. In Britain, Prime Minister John Major only survived a Commons debate, which he had combined with the European question as President Mitterrand had done, by a majority of three.

The inconsistencies contained in the Treaty can also be seen when looking at the agreed principles on foreign and defence policy. Although the resolutions appear to be rather vague, there is a danger that every step towards the creation of a closer defence community could push the United States out of Europe. One may share France's wish to do so, if one thinks that one's own interests are better served by Paris than Washington. But then one must be aware that such an option contains a bombshell for the Community because Britain is unlikely to put its 'special relationship' with the United States at risk. The Germans would not be well advised to do so either, despite their close relations with France.

Even after all of the above, the most important fault in the Maastricht agreements has not yet been mentioned. Although the Treaty gives Europeans a dual vote for elections to the European parliament as well as to local representative bodies, they are still denied any influence on the course of European affairs. Indeed there is some indication that these democratic backdrops have only been erected to hide the fact that the Europe envisaged by Maastricht is a Europe without democracy.

This fault is as old as the Community itself. People were prepared to accept the lack of democracy as long as Europe was nothing more than the magnanimous but hazy vision of statesmen, and the Brussels authority was not much more than a secretariat of the European idea. But the administrative machinery which soon grew into an unwieldy apparatus, the powers it eagerly claimed, the rights of intervention and lastly the increasing budget changed everything. The European authorities have become a centre of real power, over which there is almost no democratic control. The German government has repeatedly complained that the Parliament in Strasbourg still remains as little more than a shadow Parliament despite extended responsibilities. It will continue to not be much more than a puppet theatre where the figures dance to the strings of the only real legislative power, the Council of Ministers and the Council of the twelve heads of government.

In fact, the governments involved in Brussels have steadily accrued more and more power. They have at their disposal dozens of special budgets, hidden accounts and funds which they distribute at their discretion. The European audit office controls their use but governments deceive it. The audit office was to some extent upgraded by the Maastricht Treaty in that it became a fully-fledged institution of the Community; at least the comptrollers can now appeal to the European Court if their national authorities withhold auditing data, as the French recently did. But governments still go on giving hundreds of low-interest loans, grants for social plans and economic support programmes for underdeveloped regions, amounting to 114 aid programmes in 1992. They are able to manoeuvre vast hidden funds amounting to billions. Far removed from any effective supervision, they have thus brought about something close to a clandestine *coup d'etat* by building a supranational order; in doing so they have created a climate of suspicion, mismanagement and waste. In 1992 alone the Commission's fraud office uncovered a total of 1,108 cases of fraud which cost the European tax payer more than twenty billion Marks, or eight billion pounds. Inevitably, this kind of abuse damages the integrity of the European cause.

There are calls from all sides to stop this practice by substantially strengthening the European Parliament and replacing the Commissioners with elected politicians. But this raises the question as to whether democratic structures can ever be effective on a European level. Democracies live on the formation of public opinion, and this process demands that the people can inform themselves unhindered and have a free exchange of ideas at any time with anyone. But nine languages are spoken in the Community and the large majority of citizens are not able to communicate with each other. Consequently there is no European public, nor even a proper European newspaper. Bilingual television programmes between Germany and France, for example, lead a ghostly life below the levels at which viewing quotas are registered.

A European identity cannot be introduced by decree. It develops through memories of a common history, through common interest and common aims. Of course part of it can be created, as its resolute advocates proclaim, by letting Europe start without delay. But this is a difficult task, and so far not even a beginning has been made. The miserable denouement of the Yugoslav tragedy has shown how far Europe remains from any togetherness. Every day drives that lesson home anew.

Another difficulty lies in the fact that democratic decisions are taken according to the principle of majority. But where there is no common language, no real opportunities for participation and no European consciousness, all majority decisions must perforce be regarded as acts of submission to foreign interests. That contradicts the very essence of democracy. Although majority decisions are accepted by the defeated party in democratic systems, this is only the case because there are accords over and above the object of dispute in which the minority finds itself and its ideas reflected. It follows that Europe cannot be brought closer together in the foreseeable future without an inherent lack of democratic substance.

These and other contradictions have not been sufficiently considered. In Birmingham, Helmut Kohl once again asked the fundamental question underlying all European efforts: in what direction were the Twelve moving and where were they aiming to go? The answer has to be that a democratic Europe is only conceivable as a federal league of nation-states with powers that are prudently delegated and also narrowly circumscribed. The aim should not be to subsume the individual states under a centralised 'super-state'. Such a 'super-state' cannot fail to have levelling tendencies on account of its bureaucracy. All the pledges of subsidiarity are thus reduced to paper slogans scattered by the wind.

The conclusions do not inspire confidence. In the forty years which have just gone by, Europe was a great ideal. That ideal sprung from the trauma of two devastating wars and the defensive instinct against a restlessly expanding Soviet Union. It was a combination of hope, disguised egoism and haphazard good will. But the attempt to use the energies released by the collapse of the old world order as an impetus for political union has now reached its limit. It is the paradoxical merit of Maastricht to have demonstated what a more closely-linked Europe should not look like. The debates which Maastricht has sparked off are the first serious attempts at grappling with what is desirable and possible, and what is not.

There are of course weighty and compelling reasons for a closer union which must certainly include the countries of Central and Eastern Europe. In the economic field union is really only a question of procedure, whereas currency policy is already more contentious. But no country can by itself overcome the ecological problems, or the flood of migration. No country can by itself set up large scientific and technical projects or successfully fight economic crime or criminal syndicates operating across borders. And no country alone can survive competition from the Far East and the United States. During the 1980s Europe already fell far behind these main rivals.

These problems can only be solved if rights of sovereignty are abandoned. Unless the nations are prepared to relinquish them Europe will be nothing more than an internal market. The problems I have mentioned show that an internal market is not enough. It is true that sovereignties are becoming less and less important in the world, but they still have an almost canonical standing in the eyes of the traditionalist European nations. If, contrary to previous practice, one were to begin with these concrete steps, then the

European house would not start with the roof but rest on relatively solid foundations. What is more, it would reveal the beneficial aspects of Europe.

What is badly needed is a pause for stock-taking and for pragmatic consolidation. Supporters of integration may consider such a pause a step backwards. But a Community which is split, paralysed and has dubious democratic credentials would throw Europe much further back. Moreover every conflict, such as the one over the European Monetary System, reveals how strong national interests still are. For the time being the nation-state probably is and will continue to be the sphere of civil political experience. The past few years have taught us that the abolition of the nation-state only seems to strengthen nationalism. Maastricht was an attempt to further European integration while protecting national elements; but the treaty only shows that while one can think in paradoxes, peoples cannot live in them.

Only the Germans seem to think that they can. They, more than any other nation, have the inculcated ability to separate idea and reality. That partly explains why all the political parties in Germany agreed to Maastricht almost without delay. Furthermore, the Germans have no distinct national consciousness and are only just in the painful process of regaining one. They were also aware that they could not afford to let Maastricht founder, for that would immediately have aroused the suspicion that the re-unified country wanted to withdraw from Europe and tread the old *'Sonderwege'*. Germany also feared the nightmare of history, not so much because it had learnt more from the past than others, but because the horrors of history start on its immediate borders.

For these reasons, there is still much to be said for a closer *rapprochement* between the European peoples. But, understandably, these peoples seek benefits which are more tangible than the self-gratification of politicans and anonymous organisations. They want a sensible balance between keeping their familiar way of life and those sacrifices which are the price of every community. The widespread rejection of Maastricht is not a vote against the concept of closer cooperation but against the management of Europe which has gone astray. Jacques Chirac was not alone in finding it 'mediocre and full of ulterior motives'.

As well as cooperation the nations also need scope for their differences. What Europe is and what makes it unique has from the time of the city-states of ancient Greece always been partly due to challenges. There has always been disparity between neighbours, and tensions and even contrasts between them as well. Sometimes what divided the people determined their misfortune, but more often it determines their good fortune. Europe's wealth, and its magic, also derived from variety. Every country needed an adversary, with the border and the rival just beyond; it was only these conflicts that made each people refine its own identity.

That is the essence of the European problem. It has to do with togetherness and diversity, the one within the other, and it requires something like the squaring of the circle. Nobody expects politicians to achieve that, but everybody expects them to grasp the enormity of the task. They must prevent rivalries from developing into wars between revived nationalisms. At the same time they must ensure that closer union is not achieved in the form of a United States of Europe, in the American sense. Otherwise Europe would forfeit the very thing that makes it unique.

It seems that a majority of Europeans are finally waking up to the risks that a defective structure carries with it. This suggests that the period of well-meaning and short-sighted affirmations, which triumphed once more in Maastricht, is over. A period of reflection and patient consummation can now begin, in the awareness that the first stage in the creation of Europe definitely lies behind us and that it is time for the second to begin.

For the issue will continue to exist. We should not allow ourselves to be distracted by mythology, where Europa is the name of a girl who is raped and in the end forsaken by the gods. One of the clichés which the English often apply to the Germans is that they are all Hegelians. I am not, but nonetheless I will end in true Hegelian fashion. There is no sensible, necessary and timely concept of that substance which is so impotent as to succeed only as a concept. In the end reality will follow.

JOCHEN THIES

Germany and Eastern Europe between Past and Future

Even nearly fifty years since the Second World War, after which the Federal Republic was created with a completely western orientation, one cannot deny the fact that over the last two hundred years Germany's closest partner apart from the Austro-Hungarian Empire has been Russia. In the thinking and the mentality of Germans today one can still discover traces of that old tie. In their attitudes towards the west they have ceased since 1945 to think in terms of being a great power, but this conviction has not disappeared from attitudes towards the East. Germany has always felt itself a great country in this region, and thus as the natural partner of Moscow. This feeling is perhaps the modern version of the Stresemann generation of the 1920s.

Given the priority of the relationship with the Soviet Union and later Russia after 1945, relations with the other countries of Eastern Europe have been much more difficult since the Second World War. While it was a divided country, Germany had great difficulties in accepting the desire of the Baltic States to become independent from the USSR shortly before the Berlin Wall came down in 1989. Although it was generally felt in Germany that the country had a huge moral obligation towards Estonia, Latvia and Lithuania because of the Hitler-Stalin Pact of 1939, the government was reluctant to put pressure on Mikhail Gorbachev. In the present very emotional situation in the Baltic States with their sentiments against the Russian minorities and the presence of Russian troops, it should not be forgotten either that there was already an element of self-destruction in those young democracies before the two dictators wiped them from the map. The fascism which was on the rise in this

65

part of Europe, as in many other places, between the wars cannot be explained and understood without referring to the strong German element in the upper middle classes, situated mainly in the cities of these three countries which again are looking with high hopes towards Germany. Bonn, with all its burdens from the past, strongly wishes that other countries will take the lead here, particularly Scandinavian states such as Finland and Sweden. But the Baltic states, woken up like the rest of the East from a frozen period of their history, see the relationship their way, and that means that Germany is the key partner.

German reluctance to play a major role unilaterally in this area also stems from the fact that the future of the adjacent Kaliningrad area, the former Köningsberg, – the place where the Prussian kings since 1701 were crowned – is completely open. The independence of the Baltic States and of Belorusia has led to the fact that there is no longer a land access between Russia and the Kaliningrad 'oblast', which since 1945 was never a Soviet republic but was directly administered by Moscow. Kaliningrad finds itself therefore in a condition like that of the free city of Danzig after 1918. Already a strong naval and military base before the collapse of the USSR, Kaliningrad today holds additional troops from the Russian garrisons which are being dissolved in eastern Germany. This undoubtedly creates a huge security problem in the area, since Kaliningrad is very close to the Baltic countries.

The 'window of opportunity' seems to have disappeared already: it is too late to form a federation between the three Baltic States and Kaliningrad under the umbrella of the European Union and Russia, supported by the Scandinavian States. Instead of creating larger unities, every country is now going its own way with its own national currency, diplomatic service, customs regulations and national army. Will this be the future of Europe, or at least, of Eastern Europe, to have states of between two and six million inhabitants, which apart from some exceptions will not be strong enough to survive and thus will radicalise in political terms? It seems that an opportunity was missed because Bonn was too frightened to act and to take the lead.

The uncontrolled influx of ethnic Germans from all parts of the former Soviet Union into the Kaliningrad area may sooner or later lead to problems inside and outside Germany. The German refugee organisations and radical parties will discover this development as an issue, and so possibly will other countries. There is an inherent problem for Germany which can only be solved if the country receives back all those who left for Eastern Europe some hundred years ago. To help those ethnic Germans who now live in Kazakhstan or in Siberia after being expelled by Stalin from their former places of settlement in 1941 does not solve the problem, because any German financial contribution creates the fact of inequality between Russia and other states. The history of the first half of the century still is very fresh in the minds of the peoples in Eastern Europe. Possible German courses of action are therefore limited, but are not completely restricted.

This may also be true for the most difficult relationship in Eastern Europe, that between Germany and Poland. Although the border problems seem now to have been solved, the relationship still suffers thanks to the German role in Poland since the eighteenth century, which contributed, along with cooperation from Russia and Austria, to the complete disappearance of that country from the map. Much more important for our own time was the German occupation during the Second World War. When compared with other countries, even with the Soviet Union, Poland had proportionally the highest losses of any among its civilian population; and even these are overshadowed by the fact that the Holocaust took place primarily on Polish soil. Auschwitz is never forgotten.

The loss of the southern part of East Prussia, Silesia and Pomerania with the expulsion of millions of Germans after 1945 has led on the German side to a form of self-justification, of balancing what has happened between 1939 and 1945 and after. It should never be forgotten, however, that it was the Germans who started that avalanche of cruelties followed by revanche. The relationship remains a difficult one; it cannot be compared with the situation between Germany and France after the Second World War. The reconciliation launched by Konrad Adenauer and Charles de Gaulle was easier because fewer atrocities had been committed during the German occupation of France or during the French occupation in the southwest of Germany between 1945 and 1949. And, possibly more importantly, Germany and France were, when the treaty of friendship was signed in 1963, on equal terms economically. Today the economic inequality between Germany and Poland seems to be the biggest problem. The East Germans receive a huge transfer of wealth from the western part of the country, but the Poles do not. Natural feelings of pride are undermined by poor economic performance. Poland feels that it is on the other shore of a European Rio Grande, represented

by the Oder-Neisse border, which divides the rich part of Europe from
the poor one.

Relations with the Czech Republic are by comparison easier.
Certainly there is also a historical problem with the memories of the
destruction of the post-World War I republic by the Germans in 1938,
the occupation which followed, and Lidice. There are on the other
side the *Sudentendeutschen*, mainly living today in Bavaria, who are less
accepting of the expulsions than are other refugee groups probably
because they were farmers and still feel attached to their land and
property. But the basis of the relationship between Germany and the
Czech Republic is a solid one. Already before 1989, Vaclav Havel
figured in Germany as one of the impressive, charismatic leaders
which the east – with the exception of East Germany – was able to
produce. And the general assessment is that the Czechs will be the
first in Eastern Europe to have an economic take-off. There is a
general confidence that the advanced industrial society of the 1920s
and 1930s will soon return. This confidence may have led to the early
and ambitious German investment plans, led by Volkswagen, which
unfortunately under the present climate of economic restrictions
have tended to be reduced or to disappear. There is at the moment
no fear in Prague of German economic engagement in the country;
if such a fear arises it will be nurtured by the fact that the
Sudentendeutschen are still bringing forward their claims, and that the
old communists have an interest in inflating rumours of a greater
Germany which is putting the future of the country into question.

All the other countries of Eastern Europe are, with the exception
of Hungary, out of reach for different reasons. Slovakia, which
became independent in 1993, was a product of Germany under the
Nazis, during the better days of the regime a forgotten ally of minor
status. Later it was occupied and in the days of the communists
became a huge military production machine. The problems of
Bratislava today are manifold. The German government does not
like to see this fragile government going in a dangerous, populist
direction, doing harm to the relationship with the strong Hungarian
minority in the country. There is also some nervousness in Bonn over
Slovak efforts to whitewash the reputations of those who collaborated
with the Hitler regime.

The best relationship between Germany and an Eastern European
state is that which exists between Bonn and Budapest. The Federal
Republic was already assisting Hungary before the crucial year of
1989, which explains why the Hungarian government did not

cooperate with the Honecker regime; this in turn led to the end of the isolation of East Germany when the Hungarian Iron Curtain was dismantled in the spring of 1989. Everyone who realised how many East Germans took their summer vacation in Hungary, the East German 'Italy', or in Yugoslavia, knew that a fair number would not return. The exodus of the youngest and brightest was too much for the Honecker regime. The Hungarians contributed greatly to this development, possibly thanks to their long familiarity with the Germans and links with Austria.

Even Romania, another ally of Germany during the Second World War, is not high on the agenda these days. The main reason again is that Germany is overwhelmed by its internal problems and priorities, but there is another important factor: the exodus of the ethnic Germans who for centuries had lived in two major settlements in Romania. These had already begun to leave the country in the days of Nicolae Ceaucescu, when the West German government payed Romania a premium per capita as it did for East German expatriates. But even when Romania, after the death of its dictator, started on its difficult path to become a democracy, the patience of the German minority had gone. With the exception of several thousands, mostly old people, hundreds of thousands left the country within two years, thus bringing to an end German colonisation of Eastern Europe in this area.

Without nostalgia or irredentism, it can be seen that the exodus of minorities which started in the Second World War continues. When will it come to an end, or is the collapse of Yugoslavia only the prelude to a new chapter? Bulgaria, although the classical ally of Russia over the decades, is now a good but distant partner of Germany. There is a certain relief in Bonn that this country, even without much sympathy or help, is on the way to recovery from forty years under a communist regime. Its president and philosopher has some support in Germany, but Sofia is too far away from Germany these days. And the war in former Yugoslavia has contributed to the fact that Bulgaria, like many other countries of the former communist bloc, is a forgotten place.

This is not so much the case with Albania, which under Enver Hoxha was the most unknown part of Europe. Germany gave considerable financial support when democracy was born in the land of the Skipetars who, during the Second World War, were occupied by the Italians. Italy was of course after the end of communism the place of attraction for many Albanians; over twenty thousand

Albanians came by ship to the Italian shore, because they had watched Italian TV in their prison. The Italian government sent most of them back, but several thousands came to Germany, contributing heavily to a new and unknown type of criminality among the asylum-seekers. Life is difficult for the foreigners from Eastern Europe in Germany and the crime rate is extremely high among the Albanians and the Romanians; this is a problem which cannot easily be solved.

Yugoslavia, or what remains of Tito's country, is a special case. First and foremost, one has to be surprised that Yugoslavia is no longer attracting public interest in Germany. Since the early 1960s Yugoslavia was for both Germanies a low budget holiday country. Millions of Germans came to profit from the hospitality of the friendly peoples along the Adriatic shore. But those days were forgotten when the war broke out, despite the fact that a strong group of some 800,000 Yugoslavs, mostly Croats, is living in Germany.

The German government then made the mistake of going for an early recognition of Slovenia and Croatia, putting pressure on its partners in the European Community and thus creating many second thoughts among friends and allies. But, so soon after the unification, Bonn was not going to go back to the past or to the pre-war period. It did not seek political hegemony and economic penetration of the Balkans, or try to throw its weight around, as some of its critics wrote. On the contrary, there was only a deep feeling that other countries in Europe also deserved the right of self-determination which had been given to Germany only a few months before. But this also meant that Germany, with some innocence and some naiveté, became involved in the problems of the Balkans. Recognition was not enough; it even increased tensions in Croatia, where not enough attention was given to the Serbian minority.

Conflict on a large scale was therefore inevitable. Step by step Germany went back from a forward position to a position as a mere observer, leaving the principal place to the French and the British who here found an early compensation for what they had lost in the two-plus-four process. Britain and France, together with other countries, sent large contingents of blue helmets, whereas the Germans, using a false historical argument, preferred to stay out. As with the Baltic countries, Germany is trying to look away from a problem which is on its doorstep. But, as in the Gulf War, sooner or later the greater share of the bill will show up on the German side; for the reconstruction of the country, for example. Moreover, the historical argument is far from being convincing. If the country cannot play a role in a place where German soldiers were active during the Second World War, where on earth can Germany then be a partner now and in the near future? Where can it participate in risk-sharing and where will it demonstrate solidarity with others? If one looks at the map of Europe in 1942 it is clear that Germany must sooner or later abandon this unconvincing argument; the Third Reich then was at its peak, conquering Europe between Brest and the Channel Islands and the Caucasus, between the Nord Cap and Libya. If Bonn seriously takes the past so literally, military help is only possible in England and Ireland.

A military role for Germany alongside other European nations and countries like Canada, with an outstanding record of peace-keeping, is also important for another reason. If the philosophy of 'never again', which after 1945 has been the lesson for the country of the Holocaust, is taken seriously, then the Germans cannot stand by and witness killings, mass violations and warfare of the type which is dominating many places in the Balkans. The lesson of the past has to be for Germany to read and to understand some of the parallels of the 1930s in our time. When Hitler marched into the Rhineland in March 1936, the price of stopping him would have been low compared with what the whole world had to invest after 1939. The same may be true for different reasons in the Balkans. Many see Yugoslavia and what has happened there during the last two years as something which will be repeated on a much larger scale one day in Russia. An end to the killing in former Yugoslavia is therefore in the best interests of Germany.

If the war goes on, the old coalition could emerge in a new form; the Entente powers from ancient times will be the ones which deploy troops and Germany, Austria and Hungary will be the civilian powers which provide humanitarian aid and shelter for the millions to come when the basis of life in the Balkans is finally destroyed. A too pessimistic scenario? It may even get worse, when additional crises emerge for the island of wealth which the European Union represents. The southern rim of the Mediterranean is menacing France, Spain and Italy. What will happen if Algeria goes out of control and Morocco and Egypt follow? Who will care for the millions of refugees? But solidarity, finding a common answer to the poverty migration from the East which is already taking place, is an unknown word in Western Europe. Germany recently altered its asylum law. Soon after, small countries like the Netherlands felt the effects, but the German government was able to declare to its own people that the numbers of asylum seekers had gone down. The fact is that liberal democracies cannot promise to bring migration down to zero; this is a zero sum game.

What are the lessons Germany has to draw from the new situation in Eastern Europe, overshadowing the miracle of 1989 with its peaceful revolution which swept away the dictators overnight? History starts to matter again. Germany cannot escape from it, nor can the country run away from the new realities of geography. There is no relief from being positioned in the middle of Europe. Germany has to accept the fact and must act in order to overcome the traumatic memories of the past when the middle position after Bismarck led to great European wars, bringing to an end the history of the German Reich, founded in 1871, after just two generations in 1945.

But Germany must also be aware that it has now entered a time of difficult choices. Western integration has to go together with German initiatives for the East. And here the problems might increase in importance and amplitude to such an extent that Bonn, or very soon Berlin, will have to act even when other European partners do not follow. The shocking conclusion of 1989 and the collapse of the USSR when seen from a power perspective is that, as the German historian Hillgruber has remarked, Germany is back to the hidden semi-hegemonial position of 1871. And, as after 1890, the question is once more whether the political class of Germany is intelligent and internationally-minded enough to handle the new vessel. Overnight, the political parties in Bonn have had to go from river navigation to sailing the high seas. Germany has to be lucky this time, because the country also has an obligation to do better for the sake of Europe.

The future is open; nothing is irreversible. Predictions cannot easily be made. What we know is that Germany until 1945 was more orientated towards the East than to the West. For the GDR that was even true until 1989-90. Which line of tradition is now the stronger one? Are the experiences of the Bonn Republic between 1949-90, the general western orientation, now so solid that they can withstand a period of serious turbulence inside and outside Germany? And perhaps more importantly, what is the general perception of the new situation in France and in the United Kingdom? Will there be a common 'Ostpolitik' in the next years or will Paris and London take a wait-and-see position? Will Germany be left alone when questions are arising such as financial aid or, as has already been described, aid for refugees? Are the governments and the societies in these neighbouring countries able to understand the speed of the processes which require a sudden adjustment to the situation which the Maastricht treaties also did not foresee? Or will resentment at being losers in the historic process prove stronger?

How will France and Great Britain digest the fact that three elements of their own former power – to be one of the Big Four in Germany, to be present in the divided city of Berlin, and to be a nuclear power – have disappeared? The latter will remain true for some time, but what is its value in a post-nuclear age? Finally, the permanent seat on the UN security council may lose its importance when new members join. How will all this affect the political classes in Germany's partner countries who do think more historically than the Germans who, for their part, believe that their record after 1949 is good enough to let them forget about the past? The memory of states is long, and the myths are more deeply enshrined in the minds of the elites than many Germans hope.

These reflections necessarily bring us back to the key problem of how Germany will set its priorities in Eastern Europe between the East Europeans – who long to be part of the West – and Russia. As was pointed out earlier, Germany in this part of the world unconsciously still sees itself as a great power. Since the days of Adenauer's first trip to Moscow in 1955, Russia was the key to all other topics. Germany thus lost sight of the developments of the societies in Eastern Europe with this state-to-state attitude, as Timothy Garton Ash has rightly pointed out. The rest of Eastern Europe was for many years therefore more a cultural domain and less of a political one. To mention another demographic aspect of the country, millions of middle-aged people with vivid memories of the East did not welcome the idea of reconciliation with Poland, which was recommended by some intellectual groups; these included prominent figures like Countess Marion Dönhoff. 'Ostpolitik' became accepted only when the refugees grew older and no longer played a dominant role in the political parties and in society.

The key problem for Germany now, as 'Ostpolitik' has become commonly accepted, is to create a hierarchy of interests in Europe. From a historical, moral and political perspective Poland, the Czech Republic and Hungary matter for Germany more than Russia. They represent in a way a threefold 'cordon sanitaire' for Germany, a term which, however, has a different meaning than it had when used in the 1920s. The three countries are a buffer against surprise attacks from Russia, against incidents of the Chernobyl type and, most importantly, against poverty migration from the former states of the USSR.

This is, of course, an approach which many in Eastern Europe may call cynical. But it permits Germany to climb the ladder to another world which one may call the spiritual world of a common Europe.

But before entering this world, which Vaclav Havel recently described in the European Parliament in Strasbourg, some remarks about Russia should be made. Russia cannot be stabilised from the west. The task is too big for all of us, because we must never forget that we have to deal with a continent, not with a single country. The general lateness of Russia, the omission of something which one may call a 'Renaissance', a completely different experience since the late days of the Roman Empire, the catastrophe after 1917, the erection of a communist regime in an underdeveloped industrial society and not in an advanced one, must not be forgotten. The West must therefore take into account the possibility of a long time of turmoil, and of a period of dictatorship of another type which is more or less openly backed by the Russian army. The events of summer 1991 and October 1993 are pointing in this direction. Boris Yeltsin is apparently not a fit man, and is already dependent on his generals. The rise of Zhirinovski has led to a complete stand-still of economic reforms. Russia is no longer meeting the demands which institutions such as the World Bank, the International Monetary Fund and the members of the G7 group have set. The printing machines for money are running again. Hyperinflation will heat up the conflicts between an overwhelming majority of have-nots and a small group of extreme winners.

The future of the Ukraine and of Belorusia is open. Both countries might lose their independence again as they did in the 1920s when the peace of Brest-Litovsk created in some ways a similar situation. The capacity for statehood seems to be underdeveloped in the new CIS republics. And military conflicts at the southern periphery of the former USSR have already led, as in Georgia, to the intervention of the Russian army which may end with a re-absorption of these areas into Russia.

Help for Russia may require centuries. Support may only be effective when it comes from larger bodies, such as whole continents. Germany certainly must stay friendly towards Russia, but a joint effort has to come from Western Europe, from the United States, from Canada with its 'Nordic' experience as a capitalist country, and of course from Japan.

As in the Balkans, Germany seems to follow the politics of the West towards Russia. But even with America, German interests may not necessarily coincide. Washington has a clear short-term interest to get hold of and control the nuclear potential of the former USSR, now spread over half a dozen successor countries. Strobe Talbott, the new deputy foreign secretary, is heading a school of analysts who give a clear priority to the relationship with Russia. This may be right for a superpower, but whether it is a good approach for Germany is doubtful.

There will in any case be a new situation for Germany when the last Russian soldier leaves the country in August 1994. Then the new situation for Germany will be even clearer, coming together with a change of personnel in the political leadership of the country. A new generation of German politicians is rising and has to come to power. The generation of the *Ostpolitiker* is about to retire. Many of them had a special type of socialisation; one only has to think back to the times of the pathfinders in the 1960s, when bankers and industrialists opened the way to the East. The chairman of the Deutsche Bank, Christians, was a typical example for this group with strong emotional ties to Russia. Many of them, President von Weizsäcker included, had fought as soldiers in the 'Barbarossa' campaign. Others had passed many years as prisoners of war in Russia. Without this background one cannot understand the special relationship which was there even when Helmut Schmidt and Leonid Brezhnev met. Schmidt also had fought before Moscow, and in German uniform he had seen the towers of the Kremlin.

This type of strong personal attachment is now disappearing, and little is known about what the younger politicians think about the East. Most of them have travelled only in the West. Many were and are reluctant to travel to the United States because the 'Vietnam syndrome' is still alive. One should therefore pay attention to those politicians who come from the new *Bundesländer*. They have excellent knowledge of the countries of Eastern Europe; but unfortunately their knowledge is not being used. Only the German armed forces have taken over a considerable number of officers from the National People's Army (NVA); the German Foreign Office has not done the same with ex-GDR diplomats, with the result that when the USSR collapsed there were not enough specialists to be sent to the new republics.

Generally speaking there is astonishingly little expertise in

Germany about the developments in Russia. The old school of analysts was unable to forecast events, so that there is only a handful of top class people in some of the think tanks in Germany like the *Bundesinstitut für Ostwissenschaften* in Cologne and the Foundation for Science and Politics in Ebenhausen near Munich. Only German industry was clever enough to engage East Germans who know the countries of the former COMECON, ranging from Poland to Vietnam. To see Poland, the Czech Republic and Hungary only in the role of a new type of 'cordon sanitaire' for Germany and the rest of Western Europe is certainly not enough. Understanding Eastern Europe helps to explain how privileged the situation of Germany and the West of Europe is and how shaky the future for Eastern Europe may be.

The nature of the challenge for Germany is not clear as long as the government and the greater part of the political class prefer to stay in Bonn or along the rest of the Rhine valley. But the impact of the new situation after 1989 will become clearer in the next few years when the seat of government is transferred step by step to Berlin. Here the perspective is necessarily a different one. The old division of the city continues to exist in the minds of the people. The stability of a big city, which is poorer than all the elegant Western cities like Düsseldorf, Frankfurt, Stuttgart and Munich, can only be achieved when a new type of middle class and upper middle class emerges, and these must come from Bonn.

It is just an hour's drive from Berlin to the Polish border, and two hours to the border with the Czech Republic. These are the new parameters from which the country cannot escape. A stretch of hundreds of kilometres of seashore along the Baltic Sea will also change the habits of the Germans, making them into a leisure society with a strong naval component, as in Britain. Indeed the country will move more to the East and to the North, and the Protestant ingredient will get stronger. If one adds to these trends the new members of the European Union, Sweden, Finland, and Austria, then cooperation with countries of the North, the East and of course with Anglo-Saxon countries like the UK will be closer. Exciting times are lying before Europe when the Germans and their partners in the West begin to take seriously what has happened in 1989, when not only Germany but Europe was reunited. But as the last four years have taught, presents in history tend to be costly. Only when the price has been paid do you deserve them.

One of the abilities Germany must develop is the capacity to be a good and reliable partner of the smaller countries of Eastern Europe. Germany cannot be the big uncle who is only doing business with the Russians. All present plans like 'Partnership for Peace' give the illusion of having plenty of time. There is also a general deficit of sensibility to be seen in historical terms. Oppressors and victims cannot be brought together in the same institutions; Poland, the Czech Republic, Hungary and all the other small states have to be treated differently than Russia.

Russia has to recover not only economically and institutionally but also morally. The Russians have to come to terms with the history of the last seventy years. Only this will make them free for the future, just as with the Germans for whom the painful discussions about the Third Reich and the Holocaust will never end. The Russians must give back what they have taken away when they came to Central Europe, without demanding rewards in return. And the best investment the West and Germany can make is to send people to organise communication and understanding. Germany here had a great advantage before the wall came down, because the country had already been united in the air, with East Germans having had a chance of watching the same TV programmes as West Germans. They were not only trained as consumers, they were also prepared if they wanted to look into the abysses of their own system. The Russians have to learn this. They must accept themselves. No self-deception helps and no elegant escape routes exist.

Germany can contribute to a shorter time of recovery when it makes clear where it stands; and this time it has to stand on the side of the East Europeans. The irony of history meant that German unification became reality because Poland was the first country fighting the Soviet status quo. The big earthquake was started by *Solidarnosc*, and the people around Lech Walesa could stand the pressure because they had the Polish pope in Rome who was there like a lighthouse for a new political orientation. Next it was the Hungarians who speeded up developments in 1989. And when the big demonstrations in the streets of Leipzig were in danger of losing momentum because no charismatic leaders were able to give a direction, the Czechs with Vaclav Havel took the initiative, bringing back the flame of change to the people of East Germany.

There is not much time left for the East Europeans for another reason. Change came to these places at the last minute; there were still people there with a life experience of democracy. But, as in the Baltic States and in other places such as East Germany, the last democratic elections had taken place in the early 1930s. As democracy is also a matter of practical training, it was very important to have those people who had been window-cleaners in Prague between 1968 and 1989 in office before they reached retirement age. This at the same time helps to define the task of Western Europe and of Germany. The East Germans and the other East Europeans who have been inmates in the same big prison for many, many years deserve better living conditions in their lifetime. The communists have told them that the paradise on earth would come sooner rather than later, that only two or three generations would be needed to clear up the mess the capitalist system had caused. We do know that our system was the unchallenged winner in 1989; but the capitalist system may face new and unforeseen risks sooner than we think, if it is not extended to those who have waited most of their lifetime for the change and who personally have brought that change about. The wealth of the West must be shared, otherwise our system is not humane. Europe cannot live without ideas in a world which has to possess more than economic success.

JOSEF JOFFE

German Grand Strategy after the Cold War

I.

The year 4 AC – After the Cold War – is not an auspicious time to theorise about grand strategy or about the ends and means of national security policy. We are adrift on the sea without a sextant; we are moving, but we do not know where we are. We are stuck in a time warp between bipolarity and the future, between the familiar system of yore and a new international system that has not yet emerged.

In the age of bipolarity, circa 1945 to 1990, the questions and the answers were fairly straightforward. The overriding issue was how to balance or best the West's mortal rival, the Soviet Union. The answer consisted of one word: 'containment'. As George F. Kennan, the architect of American post-war grand strategy, said, patient and judicious pressure and counter-pressure would promote 'tendencies which must eventually find their outlet in either the break-up or the mellowing of Soviet power'. This purpose dictated the means followed: nuclear weapons, globe-encircling alliances, and ideological and geopolitical competition at ever-shifting points.

Forty years later, both predictions came true; first came the 'mellowing' of Soviet power, then its 'break-up'. The simple two-party, two-dimensional chess game of the Cold War is over. Yet, we do not find ourselves back in the multi-party game of the eighteenth and nineteenth centuries. What was the nature of that game? There were five or six players then, making for more complicated combinations, but the game still had clear rules and determinate strategies.

Bismarck, unlike Kennan, had to balance and contain many

79

powers, but he did not need a plethora of pundits and think tanks to set out the essentials of German grand strategy with dispatch and elegance. His enduring fear was of France, bent upon *revanche* for the defeat of 1871. As Bismarck wrote in 1874: 'Nobody ought to harbour any illusions; peace will end once France is again strong enough to break it'. His enduring *angst* was the 'nightmare of coalitions', the all-European encirclement that almost ended the career of Frederick the Great's Prussia. Hence in the famous 'Kissinger Diktat', Bismarck formulated the following precept for the Second Reich; the basic purpose was to create a 'universal political situation in which all the powers except France need us and, by dint of their mutual relations, are kept as much as is possible from forming coalitions against us'. Or, as Bismarck told the Russian ambassador Saburov in 1880, his 'invariable objective' could be subsumed under a simple formula: 'Try to be in a threesome as long as the world is governed by a precarious equilibrium of five great powers. That is the true protection against coalitions.'

The variations were many, but the purpose remained constant. Today, however, the world is bipolar no more but not yet multipolar. Neither Kennan nor Bismarck can provide a *leitmotif* for grand strategy, either for the US or for Germany.

During the Cold War, Germany did not have to formulate a grand strategy, nor could it do so on its own. Grand strategy, in both West Germany and East Germany, was virtually a given, imposed on the two half-countries by their position in the Cold War system. The German Democratic Republic (GDR) had no choice whatsoever. As forward bastion of the Soviet Union, it was the strategic brace of the Muscovite empire in Europe. Possession of the GDR allowed the USSR to encircle, contain and control its satellites between the Oder and Bug rivers. Given its enormous strategic value the GDR's freedom of choice was virtually nil, and thus East German grand strategy was Soviet grand strategy writ small.

Though the Federal Republic boasted far greater sovereignty and autonomy, it too had to act on a stage – and with a script – essentially provided by others. Bonn was not free to choose its allies. The condition of its rearmament and rehabilitation was its integration into the Western alliance without condition. The price was the complete subordination of its forces under Allied command and the dedication of its territory as staging post for the West. Script and stage, however, were gladly accepted by the West Germans. Their security problems were apparent in the form of the Soviet Union.

Above all West Germany, lying athwart the invasion routes from the East, could not become the prime venue and victim of World War III.There was only one solution for a country that shared a one thousand mile border with the Warsaw Pact: 'deterrence'.

In the German view, war must be forestalled, not fought. Thus, the Federal Republic insisted on American nuclear weapons as well as on a massive Allied military presence in a forward position on its soil. If the Soviets would have to attack the full panoply of American, British, French, Belgian and Dutch might in the process of crossing the Elbe, if they had to countenance a speedy escalation from the tactical to the strategic nuclear level, then they would value the status quo far more highly than expansion. The essence of German grand strategy during the Cold War was to make the price forever dwarf the prize. And so, West Germany became the most militarised space on earth with about 800,000 Allied and German troops plus thousands of Allied nuclear weapons.

II.

To describe the strategic stage of the Cold War in these terms is to dramatise the distance we have travelled in a mere four years. In 1994 the last Soviet troops, which once numbered 400,000, will have left the territory of re-united Germany. Some Western troops will remain; the total for the Americans in all of Western Europe is to shrink to about 100,000 – down from 300,000 at the height of the Cold War. The German army – almost 700,000 for the combined total of the FRG and the GDR – will come down to at most 345,000, and more likely less. West German defence expenditures, once close to 3 per cent of GNP, are sliding towards 1.5 per cent for Germany as a whole. US nuclear weapons, once numbering in the thousands, will be reduced to a few gravity bombs.

These are the numbers, and they reflect a profound transformation of the stage on which future German grand strategy must operate. We can recall Frederick's and Bismarck's enduring obsession with the 'nightmare of coalitions', but today Germany is encircled only by friends. Russian troops, once encamped in the heart of Germany, will be stationed at a thousand-mile remove. Poland and the Czech Republic are no longer staging posts but buffers; indeed, these two countries as well as Hungary would rather join NATO today than tomorrow.

Thus today there is neither a clear strategic problem nor a clear strategic solution. Kennan's answer is obsolete, and Bismarck's answer is not acute because Germany, indeed, the entire West, find themselves in a curious half-way house between the bipolarity that is no more and the multipolarity that is not yet.

To understand the issue, let us look at the contemporary stage or system. In some respects, the present stage still resembles that of yesterday. The great alliance of the Cold War, NATO, is still in place; there is still an American SACEUR, an integrated force structure, a joint command, a joint infrastructure and joint training and manoeuvres. There is also the West European Union, the purely European alliance that remained a paper compact during the Cold War because it lacked the one element that allowed NATO to be effective, American membership. And there is still Russia, the de facto successor of the Soviet Union. Unlike its predecessor, Russia lacks the distinction of 'first enemy', but neither has Russia been promoted to the status of 'reliable friend'. The reasons are evident; Russia, though much diminished in comparison to the Soviet Union, is still too 'big' for Europe. It stretches across ten time zones, encompasses 150 million people, and harbours some 40,000 nuclear weapons.

Nor is Russia safely ensconced on the road to democracy, a system of governance which liberal thinking has traditionally endowed with pacific behaviour. Russia may best be described as 'Weimar Russia' a country trying democracy without a democratic past, indeed without a civic culture; trying out revolutionary economic reforms in the midst of economic catastrophe; defeated in war (though it was only a 'cold war') but trying to find a place in the community of responsible great powers; trying to evolve a more modest definition of its security requirements than in the past without a clearly demarcated national space.

'Weimar' is an instructive analogy because, in 1918, the emergence of Hitler was by no means foreordained. The First German Republic *could* have succeeded in an auspicious international setting. But this did not exist. Instead of free trade, there was rampant protectionism; instead of capital infusions, there was the steady drain of reparations; instead of community with the victors, there was encirclement and discrimination. The same analogy – meaning that the future can go either way – is also instructive for another reason; it adds to the indeterminacy of German and Western grand strategy analysed above. The indeterminacy grows out of the ambivalence toward

Russia. It is neither containment nor community; nor both.

Containment runs the risk of becoming a self-fulfilling prophecy: treat Russia as the main threat (as the West treated Weimar), and it might turn into one. Community runs the risk of appeasement: allow Russia a freer hand, and this will favour neither the domestication of Russian power nor European stability. Too much community will encourage, and too much containment will frustrate Moscow, returning a resurgent Russia in either case to the anti-democratic, expansionist ways of yore.

III.

An ambivalent threat like Russia does not make for a concise grand strategy. Is there a more definitive threat? Certainly Europe has not become more stable since the demise of the Soviet Union in 1991. There has been latent war between Russia and Ukraine over the distribution of the property of the Soviet empire including nuclear weapons and the Crimea. There has been low-level war between factions, faiths and tribes on the southern edges of the former USSR. But these conflicts, as Europe has decided most clearly in the case of the former Yugoslavia, do not pose a security problem and thus do not make a case for action. Germany and Europe fear not military but socio-economic instability; they fear not the invasion of foreign armies but of foreign masses. Yet these are not matters of strategy proper, as tanks and planes are hardly capable of teaching market economics or turning back illegal immigrants.

What then *is* the nature of the stage on which German grand strategy must unfold? The best historical analogy is with the period after 1815. In the aftermath of the Napoleonic Wars, Europe was distinguished by the following features:

1. the defeat of France as prime hegomonic and ideological threat;
2. the wary 'resocialisation' of France into the community of the great powers;
3. the residual fear of France's resurgence;
4. the exhaustion of all the great powers, and hence the absence of a new dominant conflict;
5. the fitful withdrawal of Britain, the great extra-European balancer and maritime power, from the Continent.
6. the emergence of nationalist and revolutionary challenges to the

status quo, above all in Central, Eastern and South-Eastern Europe.

Substitute 'Russia' for 'France' and 'The United States' for 'Britain' and you will have a reasonable description of post-1990 Europe. The analogy can be pushed further. Post-1815 Europe tried to fashion an institutional framework for peace entitled the 'Concert of Europe'. The 'Concert' was not so much an institution as it was an endless succession of conferences and meetings, demarches and papers that would seek to adjust and adjudicate conflicts of interest.

In the absence of a new dominant threat, Europe functions similarly. There is a plethora of institutions: NATO, CSCE, WEU, the Visegrad States (Poland, Hungary, the Czech Republic, Slovakia), the North Atlantic Cooperation Council (NACC), the 'Partnership for Peace', the European Union, the 'Eurocorps'. There is an endless ballet of meetings, summits and state visits. Documents are signed in plentiful profusion, such as the Charter of Europe, the Treaty on Conventional Forces in Europe or, most recently, the 'Partnership for Peace'. That none of these compacts and institutions really do or decide anything of import is not so much a matter of impotence, but of disinterest. Europe lacks that great, overriding security problem that, in the Cold War, galvanised attention, mobilised resources and focused national purposefulness.

Today, we live in the post-modern age where 'anything goes'. As in architecture and literature, canons are being discarded and anyone can experiment with new and old combinations. If you don't like NATO, you can try out the 'Eurocorps'. If, on the other hand, you *do* like NATO as a tightly integrated organisation, you don't enlarge it but offer various palliatives to would-be members, like NACC or the Partnership for Peace. If you like Russia, you offer a 'Strategic Partnership' to Moscow, as does the US. If you don't like Russia, you press for the speedy admission of the East Europeans into NATO. Eclecticism rules, in security policy as well as in architecture.

IV.

This holds true for the entire West, and it is doubly true for Germany. Germany, as mentioned earlier, did not have a national strategy during the Cold War. The choice of whether to have a strategy was not open to Bonn, but over time dependence became a very comfortable habit. The problem has been nicely crystallised in the constitutional debate over 'out-of-area' deployments. The traditional interpretation was simple and rigid: German forces might only be used in case of a direct attack on the FRG or the Alliance. But today, both contingencies are highly unlikely. So what is the purpose of the Bundeswehr, especially in an age where the most likely contingencies are 'out of area'?

Actually, the Basic Law is more complicated than the purveyors of a strict prohibition claim on the basis of Article 87. Article 24, for instance, stakes out a wide area of permissiveness. It explicitly authorises participation in systems of 'mutual collective security' and thus opened the way for (West) Germany's membership of NATO and WEU. 'Collective security' is also at the heart of the UN Charter which enjoins member states to contribute military forces to the Security Council for peace-keeping and peace-enforcement (i.e., combat) purposes. When the Federal Republic acceded to the UN in 1973, it accepted all obligations under the Charter. Whence it follows that Bonn implicitly conceded its legal ability to honour these obligations.

Why then the widespread insistence on stringent constitutional limits? The heart of the matter is not juridical but historical and political. It should not come as a surprise that a nation which twice this century failed so disastrously in war and thereafter succeeded so brilliantly in peace should remain so thoroughly attached to the habits of a 'civilian power'. To begin with, a pacifist posture served as proof positive of moral rehabilitation in the aftermath of the Nazi crimes. By insisting that they have transcended force, Germans can until this day hold the moral high ground against those who once vanquished and 're-educated' them and who remain wedded to the retrograde ways of war all the way to the Falklands and the Gulf.

Moreover, this moral (or moralising) posture proved to be immensely profitable. While the US, Britain and France squandered their blood and treasure on post-colonial or imperial ventures round the world, the West Germans were free to tend their own garden and to unleash an enduring 'economic miracle'. In the Cold War era, Britain has spent an average of 5 per cent of GNP on defence, and the United States anywhere between 5 and 10 per cent. Yet the Federal Republic has never allocated more than 3 per cent to defence.

The societal gains of abstention have been even more impressive. The Fourth Republic in France fell in the upheavals unleashed by the war in Algeria. A decade later, the Vietnam War similarly traumatised American society. Compared to this kind of turmoil, the divisive debates in the Federal Republic (over rearmament in the 1950s and Euromissiles in the 1980s) look like an exercise in orderly democratic procedure.

Diplomatically, the politics of passivity turned a handsome profit as well. Whereas, the US, Britain and France took on a shifting array of enemies after 1945, the Federal Republic tried to offend none and to be friends with all: with Iraq and Iran, Israel and the Arabs, and – during Cold War II, circa 1979-1987 – with the United States and the Soviet Union. Conciliation rather than confrontation and trade rather than war was the credo of West German diplomacy during the bipolar era, all the way to the Second Gulf War (1990-91) when Bonn reflexively tried to avoid an early commitment to the American-led coalition.

The constitutional limits on the use of force – or more precisely, the political interpretation of the Basic Law – must be seen in this context. It can be reduced to a simple moral: bitter were the fruits of war, sweet are those of peace. And the habits cemented by the profits of passivity die hard. Since 1993 the matter has been resting in the hands of the Constitutional Court, but the real issue is not a juridical one but one of purpose abroad and consensus at home. Neither question will prompt a clear, let alone activist, answer even if the Court rules permissively. In Bosnia, the theatre of conflict closest to home, intervention draws a categorical 'no', uttered by all parties large and small. In the summer of 1993, a 1200 man Bundeswehr contingent under UN flag was dispatched to Somalia, but that commitment was never tested under fire.

V.

Let us conclude by returning to the larger theme. Safety does not make for an easy grand strategy, nor for a clear thrust or determinate purpose. This problem besets all great powers in the aftermath of the Cold War. But as usual Germany has to juggle more balls than most, and that task has made for a familiar German response dating back to Frederick the Great's injunction 'garder les mains libres'. The contemporary version reads 'keep all options open', and that grand strategy breaks down into the following corollaries which do not necessarily add up to a harmonious whole:

1. *Maintain NATO and, above all the US security tie* as the ultimate insurance treaty against the resurgence of a Russian threat. As in the past, the Atlantic anchor and counter-weight reassures not only Germany but also its neighbours by removing the sting of that country's power and centrality in the European balance. But at the same time it is important to keep intact a continental option centred on:

2. *the special relationship with France,* as institutionalised in the Treaty of Friendship and Cooperation of 1963 and epitomised militarily by the Franco-German Corps. One part of this arrangement is fed by sheer sentiment, since it was the clasp of hands across the Rhine that smoothed West Germany's re-entry into the community of nations after World War II. The other part rests on hard-headed interest, with each of the two regarding (and manipulating) the other as an indispensable partner in the leadership of Europe. Yet for precisely this reason the 'axis' contains numerous rivalries which spell out the imperative; limit dependence on France and take care not to alienate other European allies by preserving:

3. *a subsidiary British tie,* especially since some German interests – like free trade or the widening of the European Community – are better served by London than by Paris. Hence, Bonn is also cultivating a relationship with Britain, as exemplified militarily by regular bilateral consultations and the air-mobile division (with Britain, Holland and Belgium) within NATO's Rapid Reaction Corps. To complement this triple-tiered Western relationship, re-unified Germany has not foresaken its:

4. *Russian option,* even though Moscow now has very little with which to blackmail or to bribe Germany. In the past, West Germany's exposure to Soviet military might and the Soviet veto over inter-German relations made for a 'separate detente' and a good deal of propitiatory behaviour. But after re-unification and the retraction of Soviet power, accompanied by tens of billions in ransom money, the Moscow Connection has dwindled into a latent option. For the time being:

5. *the stabilisation of Germany's immediate Central European hinterland* is the more urgent task. Like Britain, Germany has been eager to extend the shelter of Western institutions eastward, at least to Poland, the Czech Republic and Hungary. This strategy makes sense economically and geographically. Economically these three countries, above all the Czechs, are Germany's 'Mexico', next

door and with work forces that offer high productivity rates at about one-tenth of German wage levels. Their markets are ideally suited for penetration, but this will require stable political evolution. Hence Germany is in the forefront of those who would attach the Central European Trio to the EU and to NATO, while taking care not to do so too blatantly for fear of alienating Russia.

As should be self-evident, these five options do not add up to a coherent whole. The French connection does not harmonise with the Atlantic one, and the Central European option clashes with the Russian relationship. Other things remaining equal, Germany will thus pursue a strategy of diversification, balance and compensation, trying to give unto Peter without taking from Paul and to evade irrevocable commitment. Above all, and in the absence of a resurgent strategic threat, united Germany will try to do what it knows best, to act as a 'civilian power' and to eschew for as long as possible the ways of a traditional great power and hence the use of force.

And why not? When the country is surrounded only by friends, it will seek to keep them. It will want to retain a paid-up insurance policy underwritten by the United States. It will try to protect its special relationship with France, even though barely contained tensions over free trade, the role of the United States, the evolution of the EU ('deepening' vs. 'widening') and, more generally, the end of dependence on France will make that marriage an ever more rocky one. Also, while placating France, Bonn will not forsake Britain. Germany will seek to include East-Central Europe into the EC and NATO orbit and, failing that, into its own. But it will pursue a 'Greater Central European Co-Prosperity Sphere' with prudence, taking care not to alienate Russia or to stimulate the suspicion of its Western allies.

For the time being, no hegemonial ambition or strategic conflict has emerged in Europe, though 'Weimar Russia', obeying Henry IV's deathbed advice to his son, may well try to 'busy giddy minds with foreign quarrels'. Russia remains the joker in the pack. But in benign contrast to 1919, the United States is determined to stay in Europe and a mainstay of the old security order, NATO, is not cracking but merely shedding girth. The Cold War has bequeathed an enormous tradition of cooperation to Western Europe, complete with a vast network of institutions and interdependencies which is being extended to the East. On this stage, German grand strategy will maximise options and minimise hard and fast commitments.

But when everything is tallied, one truth can hardly be gainsaid: autonomy is growing, and the old parameters *are* turning into variables because the bipolar system that gave rise to them has disappeared. In such an indeterminate setting, one can only agree with Yogi Berra, the great American baseball player and folk philosopher, who said, 'I never predict the future', and, 'You can observe a lot by just watching.'

CHRISTOPH BERTRAM

The Power and the Past: Germany's New International Loneliness

Germany's foreign policy establishment has been haunted by the nightmare that Germany might become isolated and singularised. All its efforts over the past forty-five years, before and no less after unification, were devoted to avoiding international loneliness. But as international structures weaken and Western collective bodies lose cohesion, domestic priorities impose themselves over foreign policy considerations and foreign policy itself becomes a much less easily defined choreography; and Germany runs the risk of finding herself lonely again.

Loneliness, to be sure, is not necessarily nor even probably international isolation; it is not that other countries are distancing themselves from Germany, but that their links to Germany are loosening. Today, for the first time in her history as a nation-state, Germany is a Western society linked to the civilisation, the economy, the political infrastructure and the values of the West through a multitude of ties which can no longer be severed. While this was evident for West Germany before unification, it is no less true for united Germany; indeed, a permanently divided Germany, after which some in the West (and in the west of Germany) still hanker, would not have rooted its western part more firmly in the West but, on the contrary, would have provided a constant provocation for nationalist nostalgia and a constant temptation for a German 'Sonderweg' as the price for eventual reunification. Moreover, Germany's problems at the dawn of the twenty-first century are, by and large, not significantly different from those of any modern industrial state, once the serious but temporary difficulties implied in the process of national unification are overcome.

A more lonely Germany will not therefore be an anti-Western Germany, a Germany cut loose and drifting, but it will be one which has to cooperate in a more amorphous and uncharted international environment, often on its own. And it will have much to learn: how to define its interests more independently, how to be both confident in itself and considerate of others, how to accept the exposure which Germany's power and her past in a less cohesive West will imply, and how to invest not only in the existing collective structures of which Germany is a member but also to complement them with new international coalitions.

The process of learning to live with greater loneliness, necessary as it is, will be difficult and even painful. This article will analyse why the avoidance of loneliness has held such a central place in post war German foreign policy, and will identify the chief factors, both international and internal, making for greater German loneliness. Finally, it will show some of the consequences which follow from these changes for the future of Germany's international role.

One additional preparatory remark is in order: the pre-unification past of German foreign policy which is the subject of this analysis is that of West Germany. East Germany had practically no margin of manoeuvre in international affairs. East German foreign policy was largely, if decreasingly, a function of Soviet imperial policy.

The Importance of Not Being Alone

Of all Western countries, post-war Germany has been most conscious of the need to be part of a team in international affairs. To be lonely meant to be either ineffectual or isolated. Hence the two major achievements of post-1949 German foreign policy were to make sure that the country would never be alone again: Adenauer's *Westpolitik* succeeded in integrating Germany in the collective structures of the West as well as building a special, if rocky, relationship with France, and Brandt's *Ostpolitik* succeeded in turning West Germany from a target for Eastern Europe and the Soviet Union into a partner in dialogue, as well as avoiding the danger of being bypassed by the detente initiatives of other Western states. While both moves were controversial at the time in German politics, they are regarded today by all relevant political groups as unequivocally successful achievements.

When, in 1989, the chance of re-unification beckoned, it was thanks to these achievements that what could easily have been anathema to Germany's neighbours – the reemergence of a unified, larger Germany in the centre of Europe – was not only accepted but, in most cases, welcomed. It was the fact that Germany was not alone which sustained this welcome. Both the Americans and the Soviets recognised that Germany's continued membership in NATO made unification less of a risk; not only the French but the Germans themselves insisted that, with national unification, integration within the European Community would be even more necessary than before. Officials close to Chancellor Kohl report that, as early as the spring of 1990 when the hurdles on the road to unification still seemed dauntingly high, the Chancellor already took success for granted and moved instead to secure a stronger European framework for the larger Germany, later to be sketched out in the Maastricht Treaty of December 1991.

Making Germany reliable by making her part of a group of reliable states was the aim of Germany's neighbours, partners and former adversaries. Making Germany influential by making her part of a group of influential states was the objective of successive German governments. The partially sovereign early Federal Republic became an internationally respected power as a result of being part of the Western team. And Germans realised early on that the best way to exert international influence, in both East and West, was to do so within Western collective structures.

Indeed, once *Westpolitik* and *Ostpolitik* were on track, Germany's foreign policy entered what in retrospect looks like a golden era. In the West the Federal Republic was progressively accepted as the linchpin for both NATO and the European Community, with German arguments weighing as heavily in the councils of these institutions as German cash weighed in their budgets. Bonn was listened to in the chancelleries of the West; President Bush's invitation to the Federal Republic to become America's 'partner in leadership' was issued in early 1989 when German unification still seemed decades away. At the same time, this Germany which was so clearly tied to the West acquired increasing influence in the eastern part of the then divided continent. This was of course partly due to geography as well as to the fact that West Germany, beholden to East Germany, wanted something which only the Soviet Union was able to give. Yet it was also paradoxically due to the Federal Republic's unquestioned integration within the West: although an unattached West Germany would have been easier for Moscow to manipulate, the Soviets preferred the attached one in order to have a more sympathetic interlocutor within the Western camp.

Being part of the West's collective structures thus enhanced Germany's international position. Indeed as the comparison with Japan, the other vanquished power of World War II, suggests, it was the very condition for Germany's rapid and impressive acquisition of international weight and influence. Moreover, it allowed the pursuit of a foreign policy which was essentially risk-free abroad and popular at home. Its chief choreographer, Hans Dietrich Genscher, Bonn's Foreign Minister from 1974 to 1992, was both its most accomplished performer and, through the votes it brought his Free Democratic Party in German elections, its most direct beneficiary.

In retrospect, a Germany unequivocally linked to a cohesive West while at the same time seeking dialogue and detente with a unitarian East appears as an almost ideal combination. It gave a profile of reliability and good will to Germany's external activities, while creating at the same time a domestic image of commitment to peace at home. Bonn could present itself as the voice of reason in the West while leaving the risk of action to others, in particular to America. Rarely was it necessary to define German interests in opposition to the interests of Germany's partners, since the most obvious German interest was never to be alone.

True, there were times when Bonn did get into the firing line of international diplomacy, most visibly in the late 1970s and early 1980s when Nato had decided to respond to Soviet missile armaments by committing its members, in particular Germany, to deploying American missiles on their soil if no arms deal could be reached. Because of Soviet intransigence and Ronald Reagan's confrontational policies, INF (Intermediate Nuclear Forces) became the most contentious foreign policy issue in Germany since rearmament in the mid 1950s. First the Schmidt-Genscher, then the Kohl-Genscher Governments, to their historic credit, stood firm in their commitment to the NATO decision. But these were rare moments in post-war West German foreign policy. In general, Bonn's international relations, pursued within a firm Western system, achieved what must be the dream of foreign policy makers everywhere: to have their cake and eat it too.

All this is now past. The collective cosiness of German foreign policy exists no longer. The changes caused by the collapse of the

post-World War II international system have not, of course, been
limited to Germany, but no other Western country made collectivity
the central condition of its foreign policy. As a result, all others are
better prepared for greater loneliness.

Equal but Separate

The causes of Germany's loneliness are international as
well as domestic; as Western cohesion wanes, domestic issues tend
to stand out more clearly as a potential irritant to Germany's
partners. Hence we need to look first at the impact of the loosening
of Western ties on Germany, before addressing the question of why
German domestic issues are contributing their share to the country's
new loneliness.

The Loosening of Western Structures

The Cold War was particularly fertile in creating new
institutions of Western cooperation. The Atlantic alliance was the
product of security fears generated by the post-war Soviet Union.
In its shadow the European Community emerged, ostensibly aiming
for West European economic and political integration but
inconceivable without the stabilising impact of the US commitment
to West Europe's security.

In their different ways, these two organisations represented
unprecedented, original approaches to international relations. A
fairly traditional alliance – at least according to the text of its treaty
– developed through nuclear dependence and military integration
into the Western security identity. A supra-national structure for
economic interaction between a group of highly developed national
economies and bureacracies gradually overcame national boundaries
and gave expression to the vision of European political union. And
yet neither of them, despite their remarkable features or perhaps
because of them, survived the end of the Cold War unimpaired. As
a result, the cosy collectivity to which German foreign policy had
accustomed itself is no more.

Nato's cohesion, of course, is not rhetorically in doubt. Western
leaders constantly reiterate that the Western alliance is
irreplaceable, 'the only functioning security system in Europe today',
as the slogan goes. Indeed, given all the signals of instability beyond

Nato's borders, there is considerable public support, particularly in the European member countries, for retaining the alliance, and there is significant political pressure from the new democracies in East and Central Europe to accede to this Western security club. Yet the old cohesion is gone and cannot be brought back by ministerial communiques. While there is no question that the North Atlantic Treaty Organisation will not be disbanded, it is equally true that it no longer holds the central place in the foreign policies of its constituents.

The loosening of cohesion is due, first and foremost, to the fact that military security is no longer a major political concern. Instead, domestic issues are consuming political attention and energy in all Western democracies. Indeed, foreign policy has explicitly become the handmaiden of domestic concerns. As usual, America has been the most outspoken advocate of this trend which I have elsewhere called[1] the 'Japanisation' of foreign policy, but all other Western states subscribe to the same philosophy. America's international activities, as President Clinton has never tired of asserting, are a function of America's domestic problems. Since the priority of domestic policy is to improve the economy and create jobs, so the main task of foreign policy has become to assure markets for American goods. Hence the contrast between the tenacity and energy deployed by the new US Administration in getting NAFTA and GATT agreed, and the half-heartedness with which security crises like those in Bosnia or Somalia were treated.

In addition, even when security issues do arise, they no longer have the same cohesive impact on the Western Alliance. When security is no longer defined by one specific, all-encompassing threat, member states will understandably differ in their assessment of whether developments are dangerous or merely inconvenient, what, if anything, to do about them, and when to do it. For forty years the Alliance had assumed that Denver, Colorado was no less threatened by Soviet Marxism and missiles than Dortmund, Germany; now the war in the Balkans is seen, by a majority of Americans, as a European affair. The threat of Soviet forces mobilising, or intelligence reports of a Soviet nuclear alert used to catapult Western governments into simultaneous action. But a fundamentalist Islamic revolt in Algeria, secessions in the Caucasus, or nationalist homicide in the Balkans generate not one, but a multitude of responses.

There is now an array of justifications for gaining time and avoiding action. As Western reaction to the Balkan war, the first post-

Cold War conflict, amply indicated, the instincts of Western nations in the new security situations will be to move apart, not to huddle together. Hence the NATO Alliance no longer provides the close-knit, comfortable multilateral framework in which Germany could conduct its foreign policy efficiently and discreetly for almost four decades. NATO collectivity no longer shields Germany from being exposed either by what she does or what she does not do.

Can the European Community, that most innovative, collective structure of which Germany is a founding member, do that job? This was the ambitious intention behind the Maastricht Treaty; it was precisely in order to prevent united Germany from becoming exposed that Chancellor Kohl pushed so hard for the EC to develop into a 'political union'. And yet the centrifugal forces unleashed after 1989 have not spared even this most cohesive of Western institutions. If anyone doubted that the Common Market was a child of the Cold War, the impact of the end of that War on the European Union provides the most convincing proof.

There are external as well as internal causes for the demise of the Community. Externally, with the disciplining power of the East-West conflict and of US leadership gone, the incentive for EC members to 'speak with one voice' has weakened. And with the collapse of the 'Iron Curtain' which separated the rich Europe from the poor, pressures have been mounting on the Community to stretch out and to incorporate the new democracies in Eastern and Central Europe well before they have reached democratic and political maturity. Thus the external framework of the Community has become shaky.

Internally, at the same time, the commitment to the supra-national aims of the founding members has weakened. Doubts over the ultimate objective have crept into the minds of even the most ardent pro-Europeans. Perhaps this is only natural. The first steps towards integration did not interfere with the day to day life of ordinary citizens; future steps, however, from cross-border investments and mergers reducing local jobs, to foreigners settling more easily and drug barons operating more blatantly within the larger market, will have an effect. The disappearance of national borders was seen for decades as an increase in freedom; it is now seen by many as a threat to security. Thus re-nationalisation is increasingly, and increasingly successfully, competing with supra-nationalisation.

This is not to say that the European Community will fall apart. That net of joint interests, common rules, links and dependencies which thirty-five years of progressive economic, industrial and bureaucratic integration have woven between the member states of the EC will not be severed easily. Any member state wishing to cut itself loose would do so only at the cost of immense damage to itself. In this sense, integration has indeed become irreversible.

Yet that will scarcely be enough to provide, for Germany, a stable collective framework in which her own foreign policy can evolve and within which it can blend into a European foreign policy. Indeed, it is questionable whether there will be a European foreign policy at all, as nations are rediscovering their new 'freedom of manoevre'. It is useful to remember that in the Maastricht negotiations, EC governments found it much easier to agree on monetary union than on anything approaching common international conduct.

The loosening of the collective structures which provided the framework for Germany's foreign policy is both cause and consequence of the return of geopolitics that has occurred since 1989. While before that crucial year the behaviour of Western countries was shaped not by their geographic location but by their Western affiliation, today where nations lie explains how they behave. Western countries assess each other on the basis of their respective location, and memories of those centuries in which location was the determining factor of strategy are being rekindled.

Let us take for example the experience of the Balkan war which started in July 1991. At the outset, the European Community seemed united in its attempt to defuse the crisis. But that unity soon vanished as EC governments discovered, more wrongly than rightly, that their interests did not coincide. Geography and memory combined to produce an EC divided in every sense but that of inaction. Germany along with Italy, the EC country closest to the war zone, felt more directly threatened by the consequences of the conflict than France or Britain. But when Germany embarked on a policy of early recognition of Slovenia and Croatia, this was not seen, as it should have been, as a rather clumsy attempt to camouflage the helplessness of her diplomacy but rather as a plot to re-establish the Northern part of the Balkans as a German zone of influence. Similarly, French policy in the conflict was interpreted, not only in Germany, as the confirmation of traditional French designs in the region, and British policy as an attempt, once again, to balance the emerging power of Germany by the power of an emerging Greater Serbia. Once geography reappears, conspiracy theories abound and the past becomes a caricature for the present.

And yet, Soviet collapse and German re-unification *have* profoundly changed the map of Europe and the consequences for Germany's international position are real, not just imagined. United Germany is now located in the center of Europe; it is the West European country with the largest number of neighbouring states but also, and more significantly, it has the largest number of neighbours in the unsettled, unstable East of the Continent. In their current phase of introspection, Germans are still not fully aware of the political dynamics inherent in this new location. Yet it contributes doubly to the state of loneliness by exposing Germany more than any other Western country to the risks of Eastern Europe, and by the tendency of many of her Western allies to leave it to Germany to cope with these risks.

That Germany has become more exposed to turbulence and insecurity in the East is by now a truism. Hence Eastern stability serves Germany more than any other Western European country. Of course, if East European turbulence should shake Germany, all of Europe will tremble; if Germany were inundated by refugees from the East, all her partners in a borderless European Union will be affected. What differences of interest exist between Germany and the rest of the Community are matters of minimal degree, but the loss of Western cohesion manifests itself in the ability of Western governments to pretend that minor differences are major ones.

The Power and the Past

As a tightly-knit group turns into a looser formation its individual members will stand out, the bigger ones more so than the smaller ones. It is no wonder that, as NATO and the European Union lose cohesion, the Federal Republic appears more substantial and more powerful than before. And it is also no wonder that a powerful Germany awakens memories among her neighbours of those periods in recent European history when Germany was too powerful to be comfortable with and for Europe.

Power, of course, is not a new attribute for post-war Germany. The Federal Republic was powerful within the councils of Western collective structures even to the point of having a de facto veto. If, in the late 1970s, Bonn had opposed the stationing of US Pershings and cruise missiles, NATO's double-track decision would have collapsed. Within the European Community no major decision has been possible without German agreement or at least acquiescence.

But with the re-unification of Germany and the re-nationalisation of Western organisations, German power is acquiring a different connotation. It is no longer just Margaret Thatcher who sees the European Union primarily as an extension of, not a constraint on, German power. The EU becomes from this perspective both a clever instrument which conveniently camouflages Bonn's clout and an extension of its reach. When the Germans talk about tying their country firmly to the Community, others fear that the Community will be tied to Germany. As minds in Europe re-nationalise, solidarity becomes in the eyes of many a device rather than an achievement.

Of all the European powers which overshadowed the continent, none has done so more recently and more destructively than Germany. Invariably, the new circumstances of Western drift and disintegration rekindle those memories. The looser Europe and the looser West which is emerging imply not just the greater exposure of German power but also a greater concern that the new Germany might follow in the footsteps of the old. Paradoxically, it is German weakness rather than strength, German introspection rather than German overbearance, which seem to feed these concerns. Domestic uncertainty, not international ambition, is the primary context of German politics today. And yet, far from providing reassurance to Germany watchers, this seems to feed their apprehensions.

It is true that all modern industrial countries are going through a difficult phase of domestic re-structuring, and Germany is no exception. The German political spectrum is no longer as solidly defined as it has been for most of the life of the Federal Republic, with radical groups on the Right – the *Republikaner* – or on the left – the PDS successor party to East Germany's Communists – edging into local, state and perhaps even into the Federal Parliament. Hence the placid, familiar, almost boringly stable Germany no longer exists. German politics instead have become more disorderly, rougher and more polemical, with extremists entering the political battles, with former political taboos eroding and with the political giants who steered the Federal Republic through its first four decades fading from the scene. At the same time, increasing competition for decreasing public resources will become even more aggressive, more overt and more intolerant. Noisy cacophonies will be heard both at home and abroad, fairly reminiscent of the turbulent years which preceded the end of the Weimar Republic sixty years ago.

It is important to keep these changes and problems in perspective. The crisis of domestic institutions and political practice is not just a German problem, it is a Western one, and many of the solutions will have to lie in the decentralisation of decision-making for which Germany is better prepared than, say, France or Britain. And while there is a diversification of the electorate, there is no radicalisation; the *Republikaner* and the PDS will remain splinter groups. While the issue of political asylum has caused deep uneasiness in Germany, reaching well beyond the right-wing fringe, it is important to keep in mind how German society absorbed without civil strife millions of foreigners, bringing their proportion in less than a generation to roughly one in ten. And while German industry is now paying the price for years of complacency, it still rests on solid foundations.

And yet, the country is entering a period of political, social and industrial readjustment, a process in which old ties are loosened, old traditions will be jettisoned and political in-fighting will be more intransigent. Of course that is the way of democracies, and it may even be a healthy change from the consensus democracy that the Federal Republic used to be. But it is an unfamiliar spectacle for Germany's neighbours, causing uneasiness and even anxiety among those who, at the same time, must be Germany's closest partners.

In this respect, Germany remains unique in Europe. Domestic uncertainty in Italy is taken as normal, in Britain as quaint, in France as typically French. Occurring in Germany, however, it is seen as a danger signal not just for Germans but for Europe as a whole. While post-war Germany's integration into the West is accepted, memories of her pre-war past only lie dormant, to be awakened every time things stir in Germany.

Germany's future image will thus be shaped by her new weight and her old past. German influence will be less discreet and German power will be more visible; and, it can easily become more resented by those abroad who appeal for this influence and power, as well as by those who oppose it.

Learning to Live with Loneliness

In the lives of human beings, greater loneliness is the price for growing up. It may be the same in the life of nations. Post-war Germany has enjoyed, in its Western part at least, a relatively benign childhood and adolescence, protected from dangers as well as from having to assume too much responsibility of its own by the cohesive collectivity of the West. United Germany will have to learn to address new challenges in the knowledge that her own contribution may be

the decisive condition for meeting them at all; and this will have to
imply the readiness also to exert leadership. She will have to avoid
being mesmerised by the fear of loneliness. That, too, is the price of
growing up.

Of course, loneliness will not be Germany's choice. There will on
the contrary, be a deeply ingrained preference by present as well as
future generations of political leaders to pursue German interests
within a collective framework. This applies not only to Helmut Kohl,
whose whole political philosophy has been shaped by his European
and Western convictions, but also to younger, less instinctively pro-
European politicians as well.

The primary collective framework in which Germany will wish to
act will not be the Atlantic alliance but the European Union. This is
not out of any anti-Atlanticist sentiment but rather in recognition
of the new reality that in a world no longer dominated by security
concerns, NATO has ceased to function as the primary organisation
of Western policy coordination. The struggle between 'Gaullists' and
'Atlanticists' which gave some spice to German foreign policy debates
in the 1960s and 1970s is over; the alternative, if there ever was one,
no longer exists. In the absence of a major security threat to all
Western countries, the obvious framework for any European country
wishing to pursue a collective foreign policy is the European Union:
for a Germany which is afraid of loneliness, it is the only framework.

Germany will remain committed to preventing this framework
from disintegrating. Yet here too the old ideological battles between
those who advocate a United States of Europe and those who favour
a 'Europe of States' has lost much of its relevance and sting. In order
to assure friendly neighbours in the west, south, north and east,
Germany will be a natural supporter of EU enlargement to include
the remaining EFTA states as well as some of the newly emerging
democracies to the east and south east. This will invariably imply
some dilution of the old Monnetist concepts, and German politicians
realise that. If they nevertheless continue to throw their weight
behind institutional reforms which strengthen supra-national
elements at the expense of national vetos, it will be because of a
pragmatic concern with the effectiveness of common decision-
making, not because of any ideological commitment. Indeed, one of
the reasons why Helmut Kohl has continuously favoured the
accession of North European countries to the Community has been
to make majority decisions which might go against Germany more
difficult to achieve.

A European Union made less cohesive by enlargement and renationalisation will not, however, be sufficient to provide an exclusive operating system for German foreign policy. There will in addition be an attempt to maintain old and build new coalitions, both within and beyond the Union membership. In the first instance, this will mean an ever closer relationship with France. Some have argued that, with the end of Germany's division, the Federal Republic has become less dependent on her newly-won ally to the West. The contrary, however, seems more likely. For as long as Germany gives priority in her international dealings to working with others rather than working alone, France as the only major West European country which has consistently given priority to her relationship with Bonn becomes an even more indispensible partner. It is true that there have been many ups and downs in the Franco-German *entente principale*, but these cannot remove the fact that the interchange between Bonn and Paris has acquired over the years a degree of depth, frequency, and intimacy which is unknown in the relationships of any other two European countries. It is, moreover, a relationship which is highly popular in both countries and likely to remain so.

Germany will also seek to fashion other, less familiar coalitions to combat loneliness, with the North Europeans, with Poland, and possibly with Turkey for a mixture of geographic, historic and strategic reasons. And there will be a desire, based on mutuality, to retain a favoured relationship with the United States and a special relationship with Russia.

The above describes the form more than the substance, of course. If, in the past, collectivity was for Germany not just a method but also the chief ingredient of policy, this will no longer be the case; German political leaders will have explicitly to define German interests and the German political debate will have to agonise and even polarise over them. The method no longer defines the substance. This will be an unfamiliar exercise both for the Germans who engage in it and for the foreigners who watch it. And yet to pretend, as Germans themselves tend to do, that the very notion of national interest is novel and even dangerous to them is to fall victim to a convenient myth. In the past it was not an abdication of, but a realisation of German national interests which led Bonn firmly to support Western collective structures. And while politicians and publicists in the Federal Republic have long developed the habit of claiming European or Western interests for their actions or proposals, this has been in essence a debate over how *German* interests would best be pursued within the framework of European or Western policies. 'West' and 'Europe' were the convenient cover behind which German interests were formulated; now, that cover is becoming more transparent.

But how will these interests be defined in the future? How will German power be applied, and to what end? Will Germany not, as at times in the past, seek to dominate rather than cooperate with her neighbours, even at the risk of antagonising them and awakening, once again, their fears?

Nobody can exclude this possibility, but it is highly unlikely. The reason is simple; in democracies, national interests are generally not plans for greater power or the aggrandisement of a nation. They are the concern for the economic well-being of, and the political support by, the national populace. Germany, not least due to its protective upbringing after World War II, has become a fully fledged democracy in its domestic as well as in its international behaviour.

Hence her leaders will be not adventurous but cautious. Their instinct will be not to promote German power but to assure German living standards, and to avoid being out of touch with domestic public opinion. Bonn's no doubt short-sighted and much maligned rush to have Slovenia and Croatia recognised by the European Community in December 1991 was a case in point; the reason behind this move was not any great power game, as some have suggested, but primarily the pressure of public opinion 'to do something' and the rather naive notion of the German foreign minister of the time that such recognition would provide to these former Yugoslav Republics the protection of being a member of the United Nations. No public in Western democracies, and the German one is no exception, will be willing to exchange well-being for such elusive notions as power, or to exchange peace for war. This is no guarantee against wrong decisions, but it acts as a powerful constraint on the kind of decisions which pushed Germany and Europe into the wars of the past.

Thus the real problem for German power in the future will not be how to constrain but how to generate ways to use it, how to get Germans to think of their contribution as essential for the common good, and how to make them understand and accept a responsibility for leadership as the major power in West and Central Europe. This will require restraint and confidence at the same time: it needs recognition that leadership is most effective through persuasion, not imposition, and confidence that, to quote Italian scholar Gian Enrico Rusconi, 'Germany has become a mature democracy like the others, exposed to all the problems and dangers which this implies – except a return to the past.'[2]

Learning to live with loneliness means that Germans should not be mesmerised by loneliness. A Germany which feels sorry for being alone can be neither a reliable partner nor a convincing leader. Instead, it will have failed the responsibility which the past and the power have conveyed upon it.

Notes

1. *International Herald Tribune*, 17 November 1993.
2. *Capire la Germania*, Bologna, 1990, p. 11.

HANS-PETER SCHWARZ

Germany's National and European Interests*

A Country without National Interests?

Are present-day Germans willing to use the idea of 'national interest' in determining their foreign policy, or do they reject the idea entirely? Until recently the term was rarely heard when German politicans and the 'chattering classes' gathered to discuss their country's foreign policy options and short and long-range goals. While the phrase has now become more common, real change will be slow in coming.

The reasons for this noticeable restraint are well-known. They have their origin in the country's recent and less recent past, going back to the founding of the German Empire in 1870-1871. When Germans made any attempt at all to define their foreign policy goals and options, the memory of the years from 1870 to the debacle of 1945 tended to make them avoid the use of the word 'national'. It seemed uncomfortably reminiscent of 'nationalistic', 'National Socialist,' and the Nazi dictatorship. After the catastrophe of the Third Reich, Germans underwent a re-education process and have spent decades tying to establish themselves as good democrats; they shun nationalism as vigorously as born-again Christians shun sinners.

More recently, Germans have had to deal with the realisation that for forty years they have lived in a partitioned state. What does

* reprinted by permission of *Daedelus*, Journal of the American Academy of Arts and Sciences, from the issue entitled, 'Europe Through a Glass Darkly,' Spring 1994, Volume 123, Number 2.

108   *Hans-Peter Schwarz*

'national interest' consist of when a nation is divided? Of West Germany's interests alone? This would have meant abandoning the nation as a whole. Of the interests of both parts of Germany at all times? This would have given West German foreign policy a revisionist tone, implying unwillingness to accept the reality of a divided Europe and dissatisfaction with West Germany's status as a nation; this in turn would have placed the strength of Germany's ties to Western democracies in doubt. The West Germans were thus for a long time tempted to define what was in the 'national interest' solely in terms of the western portion of their divided country, but they did so with a bad conscience. People cannot endure a psychologically ambiguous situation for decades, however, and in the late 1970s the 'point of no return' appeared to have been reached. It looked as if the Germans had finally accepted the partition of their country that had been forced upon them and that seemed to suit their neighbours so well; the 'provisional' Federal Republic was now a permanent fixture.

Reservations, however, mainly about the validity under international law of the treaties signed with the German Democratic Republic (GDR) between 1970 and 1972, remained in some quarters. Such reservations – expressed at the time by some political groups, chiefly the Christian Democratic Union/Christian Social Union (CDU/CSU), who were unwilling to abandon their memories and hopes (perhaps very distant) of common nationhood – would prove highly significant in 1990. In the intervening years, members of these political groups shied away from pursuing a foreign policy that served the 'interests' of the Federal Republic alone, except that they tended to reject 'national' categories altogether, preferring to express their goals in idealistic and humanitarian terms. It is hard, if not impossible, to reconcile the sober calculation of self-interest required to formulate a 'national' foreign policy with such lofty aims as universal human rights, racial tolerance, aid to the Third World, global ecology policies and world peace.

The decades of partition were further complicated by the fact that, of all the major Powers in Western Europe, West Germany was the most active in the pursuit of European integration. Like so many utopias, the 'United States of Europe' was distant and vaguely defined, but highly appealing. It is difficult to say whether Adenauer ever believed that such a federation was achievable in practical terms, but he did affirm the idea of Europe as a means of overcoming Germany's disastrous traditions of Great Power politics and atavistic nationalism. After some time he was joined by the FDP, and in the end the SPD adopted this line as well. By the early 1970s all the major German parties espoused a European policy calling for 'increasing integration' as laid down in the Treaty of Rome.

Germans naturally remained vague – and certainly divided – about just what the ultimate goals of European integration were. But it was possible to avoid conflict over what the final stages of integration would look like by concentrating on the *process* and declaring each step in it to be 'irreversible'. This also led to conspicuous avoidance of the term 'national interest' when politicians in Bonn set about defining foreign policy. Not all of them professed themselves as radically pro-Europe as Oskar Lafontaine, premier of Saarland and the SPD's candidate for chancellor, who used the occasion of the first meeting of the *Bundestag* after reunification on October 4, 1990 to announce that the 'new State' was merely a 'transitional stage since we intend for it to be absorbed in a United States of Europe'.[1] Nonetheless, during the 1970s and 1980s many Germans thought along similar lines.

Germany's history up until 1990 reflects a number of reasons why its politicians would approach the concept of 'national interest' with much more caution than would its fellow members in the European Union (EU) or NATO.[2] Yet further reasons for Germany's hesitancy can be found in the still more recent past, in the events surrounding and following re-unification.

In 1989, German politicians and the public alike became aware of the deep suspicion with which the governments of England and France – the other two Great Powers of Europe – regarded the emergence of a giant next door with a population of eighty million and a powerful economy. The attitude of these governments ran directly counter to the guarantees they had provided in the 'Deutschland Vertrag' of 1954, and it was certainly not representative of public opinion in their countries where many people had supported the East German protest movement and believed the Germans had a legitimate right to self-determination. But attempts by the French and British leaders to slow or halt the rush toward unification did not go unnoticed. In her memoirs, former Prime Minister Margaret Thatcher has documented her efforts to forge a Franco-British axis in the winter and spring of 1989-90 'to curb German power'.[3] President Mitterrand decided to pursue the same goal with a different strategy, namely by placing the deutschmark under European controls. From the German point of view this was an imposition and hardly the way to treat friends; but Mitterrand's tactics succeeded, at least until the European Monetary System (EMS) was shaken by the crises of 1992 and 1993.

To all appearances, the German government accepted the Maastricht Treaty as a quid pro quo arrangement by which it could attain the assent of the two most powerful nations in Western Europe to German re-unification. Anxious politicans in Bonn debated whether it would actually be in Germany's own interests to acquire a semi-dominant position of economic superiority. Was not the combination of demographic strength and economic clout likely to trigger reflex responses of extremely dangerous anti-German sentiment? This could not be avoided, unless at the moment of re-unification Germany also voluntarily surrendered its most powerful economic tool, namely control over its own currency. The statistics speak for themselves: compared with Germany's 80.3 million inhabitants, Italy, the next largest country in the EU, has only 57.6 million. Great Britain follows with 57.5 million, and France comes next with 56.6 million. The figures that most concern Germany's neighbours, however, are economic; in 1992, when the country had entered a sharp recession, Germany's exported goods were valued at more than 429 billion dollars. For Italy the corresponding figure was 180 billion dollars; for Great Britain 190 billion dollars; and for France 235 billion dollars.[4]

At the very moment that Germany was regaining the status of a united nation and a major European Power, it decided to limit its own autonomy and to function as a unit of the EU. It goes without saying that the political parties which approved of this plan were not thinking in terms of a foreign policy dictated by narrow calculations of 'national interest'. As one of Helmut Kohl's advisers stated, the '*Staatsräson* of a united Germany is its integration in Europe.' Germany performed 'a symbolic act of profound significance' when it amended Article 23 of its Basic Law to include commitments to development of the EU and 'the realisation of a united Europe'.[5] By this step the virtual equation of German and European interests (whereby for the time being 'European' is limited to the member countries of the EU) was anchored in the constitution.

For all the reasons cited, recent German history and experience have made it impossible for Germans to use the concept of 'national interest' as unselfconsciously as their French and British neighbours. In general, German politicans are very fond of viewing and defining their country's interests in the context of a larger group of friendly nations. For example, NATO was never understood by Germans as an exclusively military alliance, but rather as a community based on the shared values of the 'free world'. Now that the Cold War has ended and the United Nations has become more capable of action, many Germans (including some government officials) are inclined to let the UN Security Council define 'German interests' with regard to trouble spots around the globe. Rather than clarifying 'national interests' first and then working to have them adopted by international organisations, the German government has done the reverse. The 'oversell' of the Maastricht Treaty at home is yet another example.

Germany must Articulate its Interests in an Altered Political Climate

The basic tenor of German foreign policy has been determined in part by a need for harmony and in part by idealism. This policy has begun to encounter objective difficulties. These have arisen primarily as a result of the revolutionary changes that occurred in many European countries between 1989 and 1993. In one particular respect these objective difficulties also have their source within the Federal Republic itself, namely in the immense financial burden of re-unification.

Since the establishment of reform democracies in the Baltic states, Poland, the Czech Republic, Slovakia, Hungary, and Bulgaria, it has become objectively impossible to limit Europe to the existing group of EU members. The negotiations with Austria, Sweden, Finland and Norway prove that the EU will not be able to isolate itself from its neighbours. Such expansion, however, is incompatible with the idea of a homogeneous economic and currency bloc striving to achieve a common foreign and defense policy, an idea which was still embodied in the Maastricht Treaty. Most governments of EU countries still insist that the EU can be both broadened and deepened at the same time. But it is impossible to ignore the fact that these are, at least in part, conflicting goals.

As the easternmost country of the EU and a country which exerts a major economic, political, and cultural influence on Eastern and Southeastern Europe, Germany is most acutely aware of this; the nations of these regions have particularly high expectations of Germany's role. The German government emphatically denies the existence of an intractable conflict between the stated intention to establish the Union as provided for in the Maastricht Treaty and simultaneously to expand its total population from 340 to approximately 500 million. Nonetheless, informed public opinion in Germany has grown increasingly skeptical and is convinced that fundamental choices about the Union's future will have to be made, probably sooner rather than later. There can be no possibility of homogeneity in a greatly expanded Union; Europe will continue to consist of a variety of nations. And, in such a case, Germany will have to stop imagining that its interests can be 'European'; it will have no choice but to recognise that it has national interests and to define them as such.

We can recognise today that the European Economic Community (now known as the EU) has reached the limits of a system that, while linking countries in an unprecedented manner, has retained the principle of national sovereignty. This has been demonstrated by the discussions surrounding the Maastricht referenda in Denmark and France, the ratification process in Great Britain, and also by the palpable resistance expressed in the media and opinion polls in Germany. For the first time the suspicion has been openly voiced that governments have created a supra-national system behind their citizens' backs, without regard for popular sovereignty. Is it possible to establish a quasi-national state without a corresponding 'European citizenship'? Can one delegate quasi-governmental powers to decision-making bodies in Brussels without subjecting them to parliamentary controls?

In fact, because the countries of the EU are democracies, in the long run it will not be possible for governments to continue cooperating without more genuine parliamentary legitimation than is provided by the relatively weak European Parliament. But the smaller member states, for understandable reasons, are unwilling to accept true parliamentary representation in the Union, and France and Great Britain are just as reluctant. At the same time, the EU is more than just a community of democratic nations. Its member states are societies with very heterogeneous economic structures. And while it may well be possible to homogenise to some extent their various systems for regulating social welfare, taxes, production of goods, and labour unions (to name only a few), this process will take decades and will certainly not be achieved within the framework of Maastricht.

One could argue that the predictable failure of the Maastricht approach – ratification notwithstanding – hardly represents a tragedy. European integration suffered no permanent setback from the failure of the European Defense Community in 1954 (an attempt at integration that was both premature and ill-conceived), or from similar reversals. The actual problem should rather be seen in the fact that, even before Maastricht, the limits of political integration had already been reached in many areas. Business groups and ordinary citizens are unwilling to follow the governments and parliamentary majorities of their countries any further; few are keen on establishing a federation. Citizens are growing increasingly hesitant to pursue a policy of gradualism that transfers key government responsibilities to the European level without giving voters the power to hold the decision-makers accountable. This low level of democratic accountability is built into the structure of the EU just like the disparate economies, social systems and cultures of its member states. Their peoples, now thoroughly roused, are more determined to keep a more watchful eye on their sovereign rights than before. What choice do Germans have but to accept the fact that their country will not be 'absorbed' into Europe after all, as Chancellor Kohl and Lafontaine would have had it?

It has become apparent since the end of the Cold War that the United States is increasingly inclined to turn inward and reduce its military presence in Europe to a minimum. It does not matter whether or not this reduction is labelled 'neo-isolationism'. What matters is that the United States will no longer be the strongest nuclear power and the second strongest conventional military power in Central Europe, as it was until the Gulf War in 1991.

The US decision will have repercussions on the relationships between the major Powers in Western Europe. The framework of the Western European Union (WEU) – comprised of Germany, Great Britain, France, the Benelux countries and Italy – calls for an integrated defense system capable of both deterrence and intervention. It is hard to imagine how this can be achieved effectively, either in the short or long term. It is to be feared that a NATO in which the United States has only a symbolic conventional force, or the replacement of NATO by a European defense community, will suffer from easily foreseeable rivalries among the European powers and will produce among the members more dissension than credible deterrence.

A strong American presence would also be indispensable to keep Russia in check (in either a cautiously friendly or more confrontational manner), should it again be tempted to adopt a policy of expansion. Neo-imperialists have twice nearly succeeded in taking power in Moscow, and after the elections in December 1993 the future does not look rosy. If it began to look likely, rather than merely possible, that the Russian Empire was about to return, with all the unpredictability of an authoritarian regime, then the brief interlude of East-West harmony would be over. But in that case the EU would be far too weak for the necessary policy of containment, and would remain so for a long time.

The growing instability in the area of security is critical for Germany, which – although not a nuclear power – would be urgently needed to defend the new reform democracies in Eastern Europe should they face a military threat. Germany's geographical location gives it a key strategic role, and while France and Great Britain would like to have a voice in security policy on the region east of the Oder, as befits their prestige as major powers, they would prefer not to take on any major risks. Such a point of view is understandable, and a number of Germans feel the same way. Yet, even if it wants to, Germany will hardly be able to ignore future crises on its own eastern border.

The disintegration of both the Soviet Union and Yugoslavia has created zones of varying size where war has either already broken out or could do so at any moment. A number of destabilised nations, both old and new, are looking to the EU for support including support for their military conflicts. The crises in Croatia and Bosnia have given ample proof, however, that no agreement on an EU foreign policy can be reached by the member states. They even had difficulties in coordinating their individual policies, and the unity that has been achieved often exists solely on paper.

Certainly efforts to increase cooperation are continuing within the frameworks of the EU, NATO, the Conference on Security and Cooperation in Europe (CSCE) and the UN, and if a common European foreign policy did not already exist it would have to be invented immediately. But the conflicts are in many instances so serious and the interests of the various EU member states so contrary that, despite all efforts to act in concert, the governments of the major powers will continue to act independently on occasion, either openly or in secret. And, as is demonstrated by Greece, this can also hold true for the smaller countries.

It is thus inevitable that, in addition to the official shared foreign policy, countries will define their own 'national interest' so as to reflect public opinion within their borders. The time is past when a German government could present the results of policy negotiations within NATO or the European Community (EC) as identical with German interests, and this now applies to security questions as well.

As the conflicts become more intense and the cries for help grow louder, as the streams of refugees and public outrage swell, the German government will be less able to remain impartial. Occasional solo forays will become inevitable, if only because the German public will realise that other governments are also acting unilaterally. No doubt future German governments will continue to seek multilateral agreements before involving themselves in dangerous conflicts, and they would be well advised to do so. But whether they will always succeed, or whether it is always wisest to travel in a large convoy, remains open to doubt.

Similarly, Germany will be compelled to consider its foreign trade interests from the point of view of a rather narrowly defined 'national interest'. Of course, this has always been the case to some extent within the EC, at GATT negotiations and elsewhere. For a long time, however, approaches based on 'hard numbers' encountered political opposition. But now, however, the predominant view is that structural problems have contributed to the recession which has hit the country hard, threatening the ability of German products to remain competitive in world markets.

This very problem has been debated in England since the 1960s. If the English case proves anything, it is that when production costs make exports too expensive to be competitive, highly-developed countries experiment with various strategies, all of which lead to one form or another of domestic or international controversy. On the domestic front, attempts to curb the power of trade unions and reduce costs in the public sector are accompanied by efforts to increase industrial productivity. Internationally, experience shows that a country will take a tougher negotiating stance on payments to the EC and a variety of other issues within the community, including development policy, multinational technological projects, military expenditures, and arms exports.

None of this means that Germany will follow England's lead immediately, but we can expect that future governments will react to harsher economic conditions by protecting Germany's own interests in the same hard-hearted, penny-pinching spirit as England did under Margaret Thatcher and as France has done for a long time. Germany can no longer indulge in a kind of generous chequebook diplomacy within the EC for the sake of advancing political integration.

Sooner or later, the need to keep export levels high may limit Germany's foreign aid and often generous cooperation with international relief organisations. The same need may also lead to a rise in Germany's exports of high-quality defense materials, which have been quite modest compared to those of France, England, and even the United States. Needless to say, the debate in Germany about the wisdom of linking the deutschmark to Europe will not be long in coming. Even though implementation of the Maastricht Treaty looks exceedingly unlikely in the near future, it will certainly be argued that in order to protect German industry, implementation ought to be postponed indefinitely. In the same connection, it is possible that Germany's relationship with the new reform democracies in Eastern Europe could enter a phase of discord if the policy now based largely on political cooperation is replaced by the same economic protectionism as practiced by other EU countries. Is it conceivable, for example, that German trade unions would accept without protest the admission of Poland to the EU, when that would mean opening the German labour market to millions of skilled Polish workers?

One set of domestic issues that will almost certainly lead to a shift in Germany's priorities in dealing with its partner nations deserves mention. These issues stem from the severe economic and social disruptions arising from re-unification. Although many foreign observers feared that a re-unified Germany might emerge as a brash and swaggering economic giant, exactly the opposite has occurred. Re-unification has noticeably reduced the country's financial and foreign trade options, and will continue to do so for the foreseeable future.

The federal government is transferring approximately DM 150 billion per year to the new German states[6] (out of a total proposed budget of DM 478.4 billion for 1994). The size of these sums already makes it appear doubtful that Germany will be able to make the sizeable payments called for in the Maastricht Treaty to help poorer EU countries that wish to join the currency union. German voters will certainly reject any sizeable increase in German contributions to the EU, since funds going to Europe would obviously have to be taken from other sources such as the budgets for improving the infrastructure and stimulating the economy in the new states and domestic social welfare programmes. The proposed budget for social programmes in 1994 was DM 122 billion, one-quarter of the total budget.

The same difficulties apply to the payments now being made to Russia and other Eastern European republics. Although their necessity has often been stressed, it is unclear how such payments can be continued in light of the existing federal debt. It looks as if the demands of domestic politics will definitely bring 'the era of good feelings' (as one period of US-Latin American relations was once called) to a close.

Germany drew on international capital markets to finance its transfer payments to the new states, and as critics have frequently noted, this contributed to rising interest rates in Europe, and thus also to the collapse of the ERM in 1992 and 1993. This demonstrated the extent to which some of Bonn's most cherished EU projects have suffered as a result of the burdens imposed by re-unification. We will inevitably see this effect repeated in the future.

The observations sketched above point to one quite simple conclusion. In the future, Germany will find itself compelled on objective grounds to make its foreign policy, and also its European policy, more self-centred, more tightly budgeted and less flexible than it has been, all in the service of a rather narrowly defined national interest. I wish to stress, however, that this will not occur because Germans have lapsed into old nationalistic habits, much less into the kind of tribal nationalism now raging in the Balkans, Russia and many of the republics of the former Soviet Union. Certainly Germany has its hard-line right-wing nationalists, whose anti-foreign sentiment has been fueled in some measure by the irresponsibly lenient policy on asylum seekers maintained for years by the German government. But such nationalist extremists can be found today in every West European country. They are annoying and often outrageous, but they remain a small minority.

The more serious problems will continue to be the objective constraints already described, arising from changes in the international system and the cost of German re-unification. A political establishment which prided itself on its international outlook and 'post-national and European' ideology is now coming to the painful realisation that both at home and abroad such attitudes are no longer effective.

Germany's foreign policy orientation will have to be clarified and coolly defined, primarily in terms of the country's security and economic interests. Whatever decisions are reached, all options pose

their own difficulties and risks. A clearer and more precise definition
of German interests does not mean giving up established
confederations or paralysing them with intransigent demands. But
it does call for a different language and less fuzzy thinking in
formulating programmes, in addition to a tougher and more alert
stance on negotiations. First and foremost, however, Germany must
clarify what kind of Europe is in its own best interest, how its future
security should be organised, and what policy to adopt towards
Eastern Europe.

Whose Europe: Delors's or Thatcher's?

What kind of Europe should Germany strive to attain? All
aspects of international relations are extremely complex, but if there
were another word to describe even greater complexity it would have
to be reserved for the creation and continuation of the EU.
Nevertheless, rival concepts of the evolution of the EU are under
discussion and Margaret Thatcher's memoirs, published in 1993,
offered a highly compact sketch of the two basic options for German
policy towards Europe.

Mrs Thatcher describes 'two competing visions of Europe', and
these may justifiably be characterised as 'Delors's Europe' and
'Thatcher's Europe'. Delors's vision of Europe, to which the German
government has been fully committed until now, has developed
increasing tendencies 'towards statism and centralism' in the late
1980s. In retrospect, Thatcher believes that 'a coalition of Socialist
and Christian Democratic governments in France, Spain, Italy, and
Germany forced the pace of integration',[7] whereby the EC
Commission put pressure on national governments. In 1988, when
Jacques Delors was serving as the Commission's president, he
proclaimed that within ten years '80 per cent of economic legislation,
perhaps even of tax and social legislation' would come from
Brussels.[8]

Thatcher's picture of Delors's Europe is intentionally painted in
dark colours but is nonetheless accurate; in her view the Commission
under Delors was 'ambitious for power' and showed 'an inclination
towards bureaucratic rather than market solutions to economic
problems'. The leadership in the governments supporting Delors
displayed 'an un-British combination of high-flown rhetoric and pork-
barrel politics'. The charm of Delors's Europe for the poorer

countries in the South lay in the payoff they could expect for supporting the currency union; in Northern Europe, businesses 'hoped to foist their own high costs onto their competitors' in the south, who until then had been able to produce goods more cheaply. The Socialists hoped to see greater scope for state intervention; the Christian Democrats supported Delors because their political traditions were 'firmly corporatist'. It transpired that the supposed federalists were actually the isolationists, 'clinging grimly to a half-Europe when Europe as a whole was being liberated'.[9]

Thatcher's own 'vision' of Europe (if the term 'visionary' can be applied at all to her narrow English perspective) was of a '*Europe des patries*', a community of 'open trade, light regulation, and freely cooperating sovereign nation-states'. Currency policy was to be independent, and the EC would be decidedly open in its dealings with outsiders. She deplored the fact that it was England alone, supported by the Dutch, who endeavoured 'to raise the flag of national sovereignty, free trade, and free enterprise', while France, with Germany in its wake, had already adopted a statist, technocratic, Social Democratic policy, all protestations to the contrary notwithstanding.[10]

The statement that Germany is faced with two different options regarding Europe needs some qualification; Bonn's political parties (both in the government and in the opposition) have in fact opted more or less unconditionally for the French version. To some extent this seems to have been dictated by the quasi-mystical reconciliation that has taken place between the French and German peoples since the war. But the French vision of Europe would not have been accepted with such alacrity in Germany if Britain had not first abstained from participating in the process of European integration, then tried to hinder it, and finally irritated its partners after joining through its hesitancy and Margaret Thatcher's petty, penny-pinching tactics. A member of an international federation that acts in a demonstratively self-centred manner will not find many takers for its proposals, even if they happen to be objectively more reasonable.

Now that the governments of most EU countries have realised there is no particular advantage to be gained for their own economies from further centralisation, the British view will probably win adherents in more places, including Germany. The new developments mentioned above made it evident that a model in which democracies surrender some of their autonomy but remain sovereign states is more realistic than a union striving for more centralisation but

120   *Hans-Peter Schwarz*

unwilling to make the leap to a single federal state. In this more realistic model, a chief task of each government will be to calculate which functions it should delegate to Brussels and which it should retain for itself. Without retaining key powers governments run the risk of undermining their national sovereignty and sustaining unacceptable damage to their own economies.

Nonetheless, it would be incorrect to call the British model (or whatever modified version of it emerges) 'renationalisation'. Both the Delors and Thatcher models differ significantly from the political system of Europe before World War I and II. One can no longer speak of national autonomy or great power saber-rattling in Western Europe today. Warnings of the sort uttered now and again by President Mitterrand, that a departure from the Delors model might endanger peace in Europe, can be dismissed as fear-mongering. What would be the consequences if France were to lose Germany's support for its statist model of integration? While France would not be relegated to the sidelines of the EU, it would cerainly lose its current place at the very centre. But such is the course of world events; sometimes nations must accept unfavourable developments.

It is conceivable that conditions within the EU will lead in greater measure than before to the forming of 'coalitions' determined by national interests. On careful examination, of course, the elaborate system that reached decisions through the European Council and councils of ministers has always resembled a subtle system of checks and balances, in which coalitions formed in certain issue areas and then dissolved again. Only the French-German axis, often joined by Spain and Italy, has proven to be something of a permanent 'alliance,' but it too is nothing more than a coalition within the EU. It thus seems possible that new realities will demand more variable coalitions, in which England and Germany will have to demonstrate greater flexibility than they did at the height of the Delors era.

NATO or the WEU?

According to official announcements at the NATO summits of 1991 and 1994 in Rome and Brussels and in the Petersberg Declaration of the WEU, the co-existence of the WEU and NATO has been achieved for the time being. NATO will continue to represent the vital core of the integrated military organisation, while the NATO Council will handle the political coordination of military measures. Yet optimists who believe that this resolution of the problem will be permanent are probably mistaken. In the final analysis, Germany will have to decide whether it is better served by a broadly based North Atlantic system of defense such as has existed up to now, or by a West European system in which the United States no longer plays a central role.

France has been pushing for the latter for years, arguing that the EU must develop its own foreign and defense policies and that sooner or later isolationist tendencies in the United States are bound to prevail in any case. It is essential that a West European defense organisation be ready to step in and fill the gap. In this scheme, NATO would serve primarily as a fall-back organisation for acute crises, and otherwise as an institutional link between West European and American defense policies. This concept is also gaining in popularity in the United States, where it matches the Americans' desire to reduce their engagement in Europe.[11]

However, the problems posed by an EU defense community are considerable. To begin with, this community can only be a long-range goal. If the Europeans were to try to push ahead too quickly the Americans, who will still be needed for a long time to come, would become outsiders and would thereby speed up the pace of their withdrawal. From the point of view of Poland, the Czech Republic, Slovakia, and Hungary, NATO loses its attractiveness without the full participation of the United States. Finland and Sweden, on the other hand, which desire to join the EU, will not benefit much from the WEU and the Americans fear that the links between the WEU and NATO might indirectly impose additional obligations to guarantee the security of those two countries. Finally, neither France nor Great Britain favours a common defense policy in the WEU, since both would prefer to keep open their options for independent action. Britain in particular hopes that in a crisis it would be able to reactivate its 'special partnership' with the United States. Still other problems remain unsolved, concerning those countries that belong or wish to belong to only one of the two organisations.

Apart from these knotty issues there are, from the German point of view, two more major arguments against making the WEU the long-term defense organisation of the EU. First, the security situation in Europe has broken down twice in this century because the United States did not want to involve itself until the last possible moment. American military presence in Europe, on the other hand, has led to the maintence of democratic governments and peace and in the end to the collapse of the Soviet empire. Second, without the United States as a strong 'balancer', a West European defense community – were it ever to be granted real powers – would be divided and paralysed by petty jealousies and manoeuvrings for position.

Thus far the German government has struggled, successfully, to steer a middle course between the United States and France, between NATO and the WEU. But how long can it continue? Germany's 'national interests' in the narrower sense suggest that it would be best to continue on its present course. Should it become necessary to choose, a reformed NATO with a multilateral defense and forces for collective intervention looks like the preferable option for Germany. Such a reformed NATO would be mainly responsible for long-term planning and political coordination of ad hoc troop deployments; it would also continue to develop integrated staff and military infrastructures. In this case the WEU would be structured as a fall-back organisation in the event that the United States reduced its commitments to NATO or refused to meet legitimate West European expectations.

Of course, the NATO option is based on the assumption that the United States would be willing to maintain a strong military presence in Europe. Since the end of the Bush administration, however, German political groups with an Atlantic orientation have been finding it difficult to get a hearing from high-level American officials. If the WEU concept were to win out – and the possibility exists that it might – then the danger of German 're-nationalisation' is greater than in the present system. It is difficult to imagine that Germany, a key European but non-nuclear power, would allow its security policy to be dictated for an indefinite period by France and Britain, countries with weaker economies and weaker positions when compared to Russia. In such a case developments could take an unpredictable turn, one of which might be German self-isolation based on legalistic and crypto-pacifist attitudes. In the middle term, the threat of self-isolation comes not from neo-Wilhelminian arrogance but from pacifist weakness.

A major psychological problem in current German security policy is represented by the political left wing, usually only sluggishly active on defense policy matters but otherwise influential in the party system and the media. The leftists, affiliated mainly with the SPD and the Greens but also clearly recognisable within the governing coalition, would only be prepared to accept collective defense planning within the framework of NATO; but they no longer accept the Atlantic Alliance as an instrument for developing political consensus, and they are thoroughly opposed to deployment of NATO forces outside NATO countries. They prefer to treat peacekeeping in other areas as a political and diplomatic problem best left to international organisations such as the EU, the UN, or the CSCE, which should in fact limit themselves to diplomatic activities. With its political parties at an impasse, Germany is thus moving toward greater isolation in Europe while at the same time complicating or even hindering a genuine reform of Western security systems. We are likely to see an increase of these tendencies in Bonn next autumn no matter who wins the 1994 elections, be it at a 'grand coalition' of the CDU and SPD, an SPD-Greens coalition (with or without the FDP), or a weakened continuation of the present CDU/CSU-FDP government.

As long as this domestic political impasse prevents a reorganisation of alliances, all plans to reform NATO or to integrate it with the WEU will have to be put on hold. The strongest member of the European alliance has only a limited ability to act. A foreign policy based on Germany's 'national interests' would thus have to see a continuation of the present multilateral security policy as one of its main goals, even under altered conditions. Crypto-pacifism and neo-isolationism are counter-productive for Germany and only strengthen the existing tendencies toward 're-nationalisation'. For the present, however, they are facts of life.

Ironically it is the German left, which sincerely opposes the 're-nationalisation' of the Atlantic Alliance, which is currently fueling the growth of such tendencies. The moderates are groping for a path through the fog that for the moment envelops both the WEU and NATO. There is no sign yet of a right wing committed to a pro-Atlantic policy. German rightists, full of illusions, have once again discovered the East. But there too the view seems to offer nothing but insoluble problems.

The Chaotic Regions of the East

It will take at least one or two generations to rebuild the regions that the Communists left in ruins, in both material and human terms. Stable structures will not be immediately available, and in the meantime internal politics and international relations there are based on what Jacob Burckhardt, the great sceptic of the late nineteenth century, has called 'the internal fermentation of the nations putting an end to all security'.[12]

Long-range foreign policy strategies are impossible in dealing with regions as unstable as Russia, Ukraine, the smaller countries in the Commonwealth of Independent States (CIS), or the Balkans. The driver can only go as fast as the curves in the road allow. Since 1990 the Western Powers, including Germany, have pursued a policy of trying to build up good relations with all the new nations between the Oder and Vladivostok, Riga and Skopje, Kiev and Yerevan, supporting reform groups in at least a symbolic fashion. Through the CSCE, the North Atlantic Cooperation Council (NAAC) and numerous bilateral efforts, they have striven to promote peace, tolerance and humanitarian goals. The Federal Republic has proceeded on the principle that, to the extent that positive influence can be exerted, efforts must be multilateral and coordinated by the Western democracies. From time to time both the German Chancellor and the Foreign Minister have appealed to other members of the EC, the United States and Japan, and some positive results have been achieved. Experience has shown, however, that some independent actions on the part of single nations were and are inevitable as a result of widely diverging interests. One need only consider the economic picture.

Germany is currently responsible for 55 per cent of all payments by the G-24 nations to the CIS; the total amount of loans, humanitarian aid and direct investment by the private sector is estimated at approximately DM 80 billion.[13] The proportionally large German contribution can be explained as the result of a policy determined in many respects by national interest. The withdrawal of Russian troops from the former East Germany by mid-1994 has been a high priority; to this end payments, as provided for by the treaties of 1991, of approximately DM 12 billion have been made. The considerable costs incurred as a result of restructuring the debt were an inevitable consequence of previous commitments made by both the public and private sectors. Occasionally interest has been shown in boosting exports to Eastern Europe as a way to help struggling enterprises in the new German states; and many investments in Poland, the Czech Republic, and Hungary have been based on calculations of profit for German industries, and the same applies to new private investment in the Russian market. It need not be stressed that Germany, with its geographical location and traditional trading activity in Eastern Europe, takes a greater economic interest in this part of the world than does France, England, Italy or the United States. If anything, this interest is likely to increase; from the point of view of the reform democracies, Germany is the logical trading partner. In 1991, for example, approximately one-third of all these countries' foreign trade with the industrialised nations of the West was with Germany.

On the other hand, it should be noted that Germany's foreign trade relations with Eastern Europe have altered fundamentally since the period between the wars. Today, German exporters regard Western Europe as their most important market; in 1992, 54.4 per cent of German exports went to EU countries, 17.1 per cent to other countries in Western Europe (particularly those in the European Free Trade Association) and about 6.4 per cent to the United States. This amounts to approximately 78 per cent of all exports, in a country where the export of goods and services makes up approximately one-third of the GNP. By contrast, exports to all the new Eastern 'reform democracies', including Russia, made up approximately 5.6 per cent of total German exports. The most important trading partners with more or less balanced export and import levels are France (13 per cent exports, 12 per cent imports), Italy (9.3 per cent, 9.6 per cent), The Netherlands (8.3 per cent, 9.2 per cent), Great Britain (7.7 per cent, 6.8 per cent), Belgium and Luxembourg (7.4 per cent, 7 per cent), Austria (6 per cent, 4.4 per cent), and Switzerland (5.3 per cent, 4 per cent). These rank far ahead of Russia (1.7 per cent, 1.7 per cent), Poland (1.2 per cent, 1.3 per cent), and the Czech Republic (1.2 per cent, 1.1 per cent).[14]

A look at direct investments reveals the same picture. Approximately one-half of the total German investment abroad in 1991 was in EC member states: DM 19.1 billion in Belgium, DM 22.8 billion in France, DM 19.2 billion in Great Britain, DM 12.9 billion in Ireland, DM 13.9 billion in Italy, DM 8.6 billion in Luxembourg, DM 16.2 billion in the Netherlands, and DM 14.7 billion in Spain. Direct investments in Austria in 1991 amounted to DM 9.4 billion and in Switzerland to DM 12.3 billion. Approximately one-quarter of the total investment by German corporations (DM 59 billion) was in the United States.[15]

Compared with this, the level of investment in the East was ridiculously low. According to figures published by the Bundesbank, DM 1.2 billion was invested in Eastern Europe in 1991. In 1990 and 1991 Germany made DM 27.5 billion available for investment. This situation improved for the neighbouring countries of Poland, the Czech Republic and Hungary between 1992 and 1993, mainly because of the relatively low wages there; since the end of the communist regime in the Czech Republic, for example, approximately DM 800 million has been invested.[16]

The figures indicate that the economic importance of the Eastern reform democracies for Germany will increase significantly in the middle and long term, but the primacy of Western markets will remain. Predications are frequently heard that changing economic interests will shift German orientation toward Central or even Eastern Europe, but in my view the figures cited above show this to be an illusion. If reorientation toward any part of the world economy is called for, then it will be toward the growing markets of the Far East.

Germany's primary interest in its neighbours to the East is not so much economic as it is political; the aim is to support developments toward stability. Some idealistic considerations certainly come into play here. Democracy and a free-market economy are seen as fundamental positive values, and demands for self-determination are viewed sympathetically – thus explaining the German pressure for prompt recognition of Slovenia and Croatia. Genocide against ethic groups is sharply condemned – thus explaining German aid to Bosnia and the strongly anti-Serb attitude prevailing in the German media and public. At the official level, however, stability remains Bonn's chief goal.

Should destabilisation in Russia lead to a renewal of expansionist policies or revanchist foreign policy, we would be in for a second round of the Cold War in altered circumstances. We would be faced once again with a threat to peace and rising defense budgets. There would be fears for the fate of the reform democracies in the Baltic states, in Poland and in the Balkans, and fears of further streams of refugees like those already created by the war in Bosnia.

Germany views the possibility of political or economic destabilisation in other members of the CIS and its neighbouring reform democracies with similar concern. As a result of Germany's geographical position, upheaval in Eastern and Southeast Europe affects it sooner and more severely than other countries. (Germany is correspondingly more inclined to help; since the wars in the former Yugoslavia began, Germany has taken in approximately 400,000 refugees from that region.) Concerns about political stability also constituted the prime motive behind German Defense Minister

Rühe's proposals at the end of 1993 to allow Poland, Hungary, the Czech Republic and Slovakia to join NATO without delay.

Clearly, Germany has a strong and specifically national interest in the stabilisation of the East. Nonetheless, it is determined to coordinate its East European policy with its partners in the West. In the long run, the security of the reform democracies as a 'stability zone' can be guaranteed only by an agreement of the present NATO countries or by expanding NATO to include them.

Similarly, a progressive linking of the reform democracies with the EU can be achieved only through multilateral efforts. Therefore, although Germany has a far greater interest in these regions than do its partners in the EU or the United States, it will take no unilateral initiatives; on the other hand, the last few years have demonstrated clearly that in many instances the simultaneous co-existence of multilateral and unilateral Eastern policies cannot be avoided. Sometimes unilateral steps can benefit the Western communities, as when Germany negotiated asylum treaties with its neighbor states to the east and southeast; sometimes they can be harmful, as the disintegration of Western policy toward Yugoslavia has shown.

An increase in unilateral activity by single nations cannot be excluded, given the rapidity with which situations can change. Time-consuming consultations are often not possible. 'National interests' as defined by governments and broad currents of public opinion will no doubt continue to make themselves felt when, as in the case of Yugoslavia, the nature of the crisis demands intervention in the form of an embargo, air strikes, or UN peace-keeping missions. The volatility of the situation in Russia and its neighbouring countries suggests that the flounderings of the EU and NATO to develop a policy on Bosnia might be only a hint of things to come.

In some respects one could compare the position of re-unified Germany to that of the United States after World War II. Although not directly threatened at that time, the United States regarded the creation of stability on its facing coast in Western Europe as one of its most urgent tasks. In Germany today, powerful isolationist forces exist which argue against involvement and intervention on historical, moral, constitutional and budgetary grounds. But Germany's true 'national interests' lie in stabilising its surroundings. In the case of the Visegrád Group nations, moral arguments for involvement also exist, along with a shared Middle European culture and history. The German situation bears a further resemblance to that of the United

States after World War II; while stabilising efforts must take place in close cooperation with other Western democracies, they must be designed to deter Russian retaliation rather than to provoke it.

German National Consciousness

The previous observations have all been based on the premise that reunified Germany is a 'post-modern' nation. 'Post-modern' in this case means that it has been purged of the most virulent characteristics of nineteenth and early twentieth-century nationalism, including cultivation of historical myths and old hatreds, folk ideology, a tribal mentality and religious intolerance. We are currently witnessing an outbreak of such fanatic nationalism in the Balkans and the territories of the former Soviet Union. In contrast, re-unified Germany bases its idea of nationhood primarily on popular sovereignty and a sense of shared history, language and culture. Germans also see themselves as citizens of an industrial democracy cooperating and competing with other industrial democracies, with all the ideological shadings and antitheses characteristic of a pluralistic society. A national consciousness of this sort no longer understands the nation in terms of an absolute value, recognising that post-modern nation-states can thrive and prosper only when they surrender parts of their autonomy to regional bodies. If the emerging nation-state of the modern period was characterised by a striving for autonomy, the post-modern nation-state is focused on establishing cooperative international communities. These are essential for successful functioning, but within them the nation retains its sovereignty.

In this respect, Germany has become a normal Western democracy. German national consciousness is comparatively matter-of-fact and post-modern next to that of the French, British, Dutch or Italians. Admittedly it is somewhat more complicated, as there is a history of imposed partition and preceding nationalist catastrophes to be dealt with. But on closer inspection, every country in Europe represents a special case with its own complicated and sometimes burdensome history. What is crucial, however, is that in none of these countries is national identity elevated to mythological status. The last West European leader to attempt this was General de Gaulle, but even that phase of French history has now been over for twenty-five years, and France too has long since become an ordinary post-modern state. In this respect, Western Europe could not differ more strikingly from Eastern and Southeast Europe.

Observers recognise, however, that Germans find it harder to come to terms with their nationality than do citizens of other West European countries. The reasons lie in the historical events discussed at the beginning of this essay. This also makes the rational definition of 'national interests' more problematic than in the case of Germany's large and small neighbouring states. 'National interest', which always implies the existence of other nations, starts out as a thoroughly rational concept: the analysis of one's own interests and the probable reactions of one's partners demands dispassionate and level-headed thinking. Interests are a utilitarian category, and the more utilitarian the approach governments take toward achieving them the better.

Yet, it is also true that emotional components such as pride, group identity, feelings of safety and security and memories of national triumphs and defeats enter into citizens' perceptions of themselves as a nation. Sometimes antipathies and hatred of other nations, and occasionally self-hatred, play a role. Wherever disturbances in the emotional dimension exist, rational analyses of self-interest will be more difficult.

So soon after re-unification, Germans naturally still have difficulty reaching a rational and confident definition of their own 'national interests'. Yet the present should be regarded as a transitional stage. The more normally this re-united country is treated by its partners in the EU, the better able its citizens and political leaders will be to reconcile Germany's interests with those of its partners in a normal and intelligent fashion.[17]

Translated by Deborah Lucas Schneider

Notes

1. Oskar Lafontaine, *Texte zur Deutschlandpolitik* III (86), 1990, p. 774.
2. The British, for example, even today proclaim 'national interest' to be the guiding principle of their foreign policy without the slightest trace of embarrassment.
3. Margaret Thatcher, *The Downing Street Years*, New York, Harper Collins, 1993, p. 760.
4. Figures taken from the *Direction of Trade Statistics Yearbook 1993*, Washington, D.C., International Monetary Fund, 1993.

130   *Hans-Peter Schwarz*

5. As quoted by Timothy Garton Ash, *In Europe's Name: Germany and the Divided Continent*, New York, Random House, 1993, p. 385.
6. Presse-und Informationsamt der Bundesregierung, *Aktuelle Beiträge für Wirtschafts-und Finanzpolitik*, 13 July 1993, p. 18.
7. Thatcher, *The Downing Street Years*, p. 536.
8. Cited according to 'The European Community: Back to the Drawing Board,' in the supplement 'A Survey of the European Community,' *The Economist*, 3 July 1993, p. 5.
9. Thatcher, *The Downing Street Years*, pp. 727–28.
10. Ibid., p. 536.
11. Uwe Nerlich, 'Sicherheitsfunktionen der NATO,' *Europa Archiv* 48 (23), 1993, pp. 664–65.
12. Jacob Burckhardt to Friedrich von Preen in a letter of 21 February 1878 in *Briefe* 6, Basel, Schwabe & Co. Verlag, 1966, p. 230.
13. These statistics are taken from an address given by Helmut Werner, Chairman of Mercedes-Benz AG, to the US study group of the 'Atlantic Bridge' on 14 October 1993, Bonn.
14. These statistics are taken from the *Fischer Weltalmanach 1994*, Frankfurt, Fischer Taschenbuch Verlag, 1994, pp. 1038-39. No major shifts took place in 1993. According to a report by the German Bundesbank of October 1993, the export volume for the month of February 1992 (after seasonal adjustment) was 26.4 billion dollars to EC countries, 3.6 billion dollars to the United States, and 3.5 billion dollars to Central and East European reform countries. This represents a certain rise against the 1991 figures, which is hardly surprising; the period of upheaval is over in Poland, the Czech Republic and Hungary, and the economic picture is beginning to recover.
15. These statistics are taken from the monthly report of the German Bundesbank of July 1992.
16. *Frankfurter Allgemeine Zeitung*, 20 November 1993, p. 12.
17. A more elaborate study of the theme of German national interest will be published in a forthcoming monograph, Hans-Peter Schwarz, *Der traumatisierte Riese. Vom geteilten Land zur Zentralmacht Europas*, Berlin, Siedler Verlag, 1994.

Notes on Contributors

Arnulf Baring, Professor of Contemporary History and International Relations, Free University of Berlin. Professor Baring's publications include *Charles de Gaulle. Größe und Grenzen* (1963); *Der 17. Juni 1953* (1966); *Außenpolitik in Adenauers Kanzlerdemokratie* (1969); *Machtwechsel. Die Ära Brandt-Scheel* (1982); and *Deutschland, was nun?* (1991).

Christoph Bertram, Diplomatic Correspondent of *Die Zeit*, Germany's leading weekly, and Guest Research Fellow at the Yomiuri Research Institute, Tokyo. Dr Bertram has published extensively on arms control, international security and East-West relations. His recent publications include *Arms Control and Military Force* (1980); *Prospects of Soviet Power in the 1980s* (1980); *Strategic Deterrence in a Changing Environment* (1981); *Nuclear Proliferation in the 1980s* (1982); *Third World Conflict and International Security* (1982); and *Defense and Consensus* (1983).

Joachim Fest, Editor-Publisher of the *Frankfurter Allgemeine Zeitung*, the leading German daily, Senator of the *Max-Planck-Gesellschaft*, and Professor at the University of Heidelberg. Dr Fest's many publications – among them his celebrated biographical studies on 'the Third Reich' and his thoughtful essays on the political culture of the West – include: *The Face of the Third Reich* (1970); *Hitler* (1974); *Aufgehobene Vergangenheit* (1982); *Im Gegenlicht. Eine italienische Reise* (1988); *Der zerstörte Traum. Über das Ende des utopischen Zeitalters* (1991); and *Die schwierige Freiheit. Über die offene Flanke der offenen Gesellschaft* (1993).

Günther Gillessen, Political and Foreign Affairs Editor with the *Frankfurter Allgemeine Zeitung* and Professor of Journalism at the University of Mainz. Prof. Gillessen's numerous publications on historical strategic questions include *Lord Palmerston und die Einigung Deutschlands* (1961); *Sieben Argumente für Europa* (1978); *Über Südafrika. Ständestaat, Rassenstaat, Gottesstaat* (1978); and *Auf verlorenem Posten. Die Frankfurter Zeitung im Dritten Reich* (1987/88).

Josef Joffe, Columnist and International Affairs Editor with the Süddeutsche Zeitung, Contributing Editor of U.S. News and World Report and Associate of the Center for International Affairs, Harvard University. Besides his many articles in various books and academic journals Dr Joffe is author of *The Limited Partnership: Europe, the United States and the Burdens of Alliance* (1987).

132   *Notes on Contributors*

Gregor Schöllgen, Professor of Modern History, University of Erlangen-Nuremberg and Instructor in History for the German Diplomatic Service. Recent publications include *Imperialismus und Gleichgewicht. Deutschland, England und die orientalische Frage 1871-1914* (1992); *Handlungsfreiheit und Zweckrationalität* (1984); *Max Webers Anliegen* (1985); *Das Zeitalter des Imperialismus* (1994); *Escape into War? A Conservative Against Hitler. Ulrich von Hassell, 1881-1944* (1991); *Die Macht in der Mitte Europas* (1992); and *Angst vor der Macht* (1993).

Hans-Peter Schwarz, Professor of Political Science and Contemporary History, University of Bonn, Joint Chief Editor of the *Vierteljahreshefte für Zeitgeschichte* and Chairman of the senior body of the *Institut für Zeitgeschichte* in Munich. Professor Schwarz's seminal publications on the history of the Federal Republic, which mark him as the foremost historian in this field, include *Vom Reich zur Bundesrepublik* (1980); *Die Ära Adenauer* (1981-1983); *Die gezähmten Deutschen* (1985); and *Adenauer* (1986-1991).

Jochen Thies, Foreign Affairs Editor of *Die Welt*, a leading German daily, Contributor to the *International Herald Tribune*, Member of the International Institute for Strategic Studies, London, and Member of the Board of *Political Extorior*, Madrid. Recent publications include *Architekt der Weltherrschaft. Die Endziele Hitlers* (1976); *Helmut Schmidts Rückzug von der Macht* (1988); *Südwestdeutschland Stunde Null. Die Geschichte der Französischen Besatzungszone 1945/48* (1989); and *Deutschland von innen* (1990).

Suggestions for Further Reading

Arnold, H., *Europa am Ende. Die Auflösung von EG und NATO*, München, 1993

von Bredow, W. and T. Jäger, *Neue deutsche Außenpolitik*, Opladen, 1993

Calleo, D., 'Die künftige Rolle der Atlantischen Allianz – das europäisch-amerikanische Verhältnis', in *Forum für Deutschland: Eine neue Weltordnung* (10. bis 12.3. 1993), Berlin, 1993, pp. 32–38

——, 'Amerika wird nicht immer der Beschützer sein. Deutsche Vergangenheit und europäische Zukunft', *Frankfurter Allgemeine Zeitung*, 8 September 1987, p. 8

Does "the West" Still Exist? – A Conference of the Committee for the Free World, New York, 1990

Garton Ash, T., *In Europe's Name: Germany and the Divided Continent*, London, 1993

Kaiser, K., *Deutschlands Vereinigung. Die internationalen Aspekte*, Bergisch Gladbach, 1991

Kaiser, K. and H.W. Maull (eds), *Die Zukunft der deutschen Außenpolitik. Symposium des Forschungsinstituts der Deutschen Gesellschaft für Auswärtige Politik am 19. 10. 1992* (Arbeitspapiere zur Internationalen Politik vol. 72), Bonn, 1993

Kissinger, H.A., 'Die künftigen Beziehungen zwischen Europa und den Vereinigten Staaten', *EA* 47, 1992, pp. 671–679

Laschet, A. and P. Pappert (eds), *Ein Kontinent im Umbruch. Perspektiven für eine europäische Außenpolitik*, Berlin, 1993

Maull, H.W., 'Zivilmacht Bundesrepublik Deutschland. 14 Thesen für eine neue deutsche Außenpolitik', *EA* 47, 1992, pp. 269–278

Rudolph, H., 'Mehr als Stagnation und Revolte. Zur politischen Kultur der sechziger Jahre', in M. Broszat (ed.), *Zäsuren nach 1945. Essays zur Periodisierung der deutschen Nachkriegsgeschichte*, München, 1990, p. 141–151

Schauer, H., *Europa der Vernunft. Kritische Anmerkingen nach Maastricht*, Bonn, 1993

Schmidt, H., *Handeln für Deutschland*, München, 1993

Schöllgen, G., *Angst vor der Macht. Die Deutschen und ihre Außenpolitik*, Berlin, 1993

——, *Die Macht in der Mitte Europas*, München, 1992'

——, 'Deutschlands neue Lage. Die USA, die Bundesrepublik Deutschland und die Zukunft des westlichen Bündnisses', *EA* 47, 1992, pp. 125ff

Schwarz, H.-P., 'Deutsche Außenpolitik nach der Vereinigung', in P. Haungs, K.M. Graß and H.-J. Veen, *Civitas*, Paderborn, 1992, pp. 483–506

——, 'Europas Aufgabe – Neuordnung nach dem Ende der Sowjetunion', in *Forum für Deutschland: Eine neue Weltordnung* (10. bis 12. 3. 1993 in Berlin), 1993, pp. 87–94

Senghaas, D., *Friedensprojekt Europa*, Frankfurt a.M., 1992

——, 'Weltinnenpolitik', *EA* 47, 1992, pp. 643–652

Smyser, W.R., 'Drei große Aufgaben sind zu bewältigen. Deutschlands zukünftige Rolle in der Welt', *Frankfurter Allgemeine Zeitung*, 16 September 1992, p. 12

Stürmer, M., *Die Grenzen der Macht*, Berlin, 1992

——, 'Globale Aufgaben und Herausforderungen einer 'neuen Weltordnung', in *Forum für Deutschland: Eine neue Weltordnung (10. bis 12. 3. 1993)*, Berlin, 1993, pp. 128–139

Thies, J., 'Deutschland in Turbulenzen', *Europäische Rundschau*, 1992 (3), pp. 31–40

Vernet, D., *Was wird aus Deutschland?*, Bergisch Gladbach, 1993

Zitelmann, R., K. Weissmann and M. Grossheim (eds), *Westbindung*, Berlin, 1993